To Marie
an angel
cruise ship. Thank you
for being one of my first
reviewers and for the
gorgeous angel. Love &
Angel Blessings.
        Patty Callahan ♡

PATTY CALLAHAN

Angel
Blessings—Believe

BALBOA.
PRESS
A DIVISION OF HAY HOUSE

Balboa Press books may be ordered through booksellers or by contacting:

Balboa Press
A Division of Hay House
1663 Liberty Drive
Bloomington, IN 47403
www.balboapress.com
1 (877) 407-4847

Because of the dynamic nature of the Internet, any web addresses or
links contained in this book may have changed since publication and may
no longer be valid. The views expressed in this work are solely those
of the author and do not necessarily reflect the views of the publisher,
and the publisher hereby disclaims any responsibility for them.

The author of this book does not dispense medical advice or prescribe the
use of any technique as a form of treatment for physical, emotional, or medical
problems without the advice of a physician, either directly or indirectly. The
intent of the author is only to offer information of a general nature to help you
in your quest for emotional and spiritual well-being. In the event you use any
of the information in this book for yourself, which is your constitutional right,
the author and the publisher assume no responsibility for your actions.

This is a work of fiction. All of the characters, names, incidents,
organizations, and dialogue in this novel are either the products
of the author's imagination or are used fictitiously.

Print information available on the last page.

ISBN: 978-1-9822-0208-8 (sc)
ISBN: 978-1-9822-0210-1 (hc)
ISBN: 978-1-9822-0209-5 (e)

Library of Congress Control Number: 2018904279

Balboa Press rev. date: 04/17/2018

Contents

Part III
Life back on Earth

Dedication

I dedicate this book to all those who have lost a loved one.

Angel blessings to them all.

Acknowledgments

I thank—

Archangel Gabriel for the morning messages
All the archangels, guardian angels, earth angels,
spirit guides, and departed loved ones
My husband and sons
My dear friend Janet
Patty's mom, proofreader from the heavens
Mentor Reid Tracy, hayhouse.com
Mentor, Doreen Virtue, hayhouse.com
Mentor davidji, davidji.com
Mentor Mike Dooley, mikedooley.com
Mentor Kyle Gray, kylegray.co.uk
Hay House and affiliates
Wonderful Hay House authors and mentors including but not
limited to Reid Tracy, Dr. Wayne Dyer, Louise Hay, Doreen
Virtue, Kyle Gray, Mike Dooley, davidji, Radliegh Valentine,
James Van Praagh, John Edward, and many more
All the contributors to the writers' workshop
courses online and in Orlando
My team and tribe

—Angel blessings to you all

Preface

Nestled in a blanket of stars in the farthest reaches of our universe and spinning endlessly around a brilliant orb they call the sun, you will find a tiny inhabited planet called Earth. Earth is a classroom for the spirit world where souls have the opportunity to be enriched. But don't tell anyone on Earth they are attending school for a hundred years give or take.

Understandably, souls want to finish school and return to a happier place. They don't remember that happier place, but deep down in their souls, they yearn to return there.

Earth is one of many planets that have physical learning centers at which they can test their abilities, make good choices, enrich their souls, and move on to a higher realm in the spirit world. On Earth, they learn to make good choices with their free will.

Some of the other planets have beings that don't look like earthlings and earthlings call them extraterrestrials (ETs) or aliens, and their craft would be known as unidentified flying objects (UFOs). They have loving souls too, and they are also attending school and are not to be feared. Each soul's goal is to pass first grade, second grade, and so on and pass the final test to achieve ultimate enrichment and graduate from all classes on the physical planets as well as the learning centers of the spirit world.

This year is the ultimate test of the guiding principles. How many people or souls of the tiny planet Earth will pass the test? Embark on a journey and let's see if the majority of the people can overcome the darkness that blankets the earth. There is hope for all those with love in their hearts.

No matter what religion or belief system they have, the vast majority believe there is something much bigger out there than mere mortals. Earthlings are tiny specks in this vast universe, so there must be a Creator, and there is—the CEO of the galaxies. We will use the term *Creator* with no disrespect for any organized religion that uses other names for its deity or belief system.

Most stories start at the beginning. In the circle of a soul's life, there is no beginning or end, so we will jump onboard and see where this journey takes us.

Introduction

Earth was dying. People were sick and facing their demise. Humans are made up primarily of water, but the water had become contaminated. Regardless of how aggressively it was treated, the water was becoming undrinkable. Those who drank it, especially the children, were being poisoned. Learning disabilities, tumors, and cancer were being attributed to the tainted water. People were warned not to drink it, cook with it, or bathe in it. They were told not to use it at all. They were forced to use bottled water for everything including their baths and showers. Unbelievable.

The air was also polluted and unbreathable. Respirator masks were becoming a necessary article of clothing. The fashion industry had developed stylish varieties to go with everyday wear as well as fancy attire such as ball gowns and tuxes. No matter how chic they looked, people continued to die from toxic air pollution. Cities were smog-laden. Residents tried to escape the pollution, but the smog followed them on the winds.

Companies had bought up farmland to grow genetically modified crops. Over forty countries including Russia and China required the labeling of GMO food so consumers could make their own choices regarding what chemicals they wanted to put in their bodies. The United States would not enact labeling laws even though the American Medical Association wanted more testing and labeling. Those in power spread propaganda advising GMOs were not harmful even as the evidence against them mounted; GMOs were causing cancer. Drug companies were the winners by benefiting from the sale of more drugs as humans fell ill. Doctors and other medical professionals tried to help with chemotherapy and radiation only to watch their patients suffer and die.

The ice caps were melting rapidly. The arctic poles were turning green with moss and were littered with animal and bird carcasses. The sea level had risen and swallowed up islands. The coastlines throughout the world were receding and taking people's homes with them. Large sections of interior lands were collapsing from excessive mining and fracking. Earthquakes occurred where they never had before. Devastating hurricanes, tornadoes, earthquakes, blizzards, floods, extreme temperatures, and unpredictable weather patterns were dealing blow after blow. Entire towns and islands were wiped out. People were losing their homes and possessions. The idea of global warning was laughed at as statistical records were broken in all areas.

Diseases were spreading globally. Insects went unchecked. Wild animals ventured into habitable areas causing destruction in their path. Earth's inhabitants were worried and upset; they passed the blame and were generally nasty to one another. Famine and drought were killing thousands including children. Plagues were upon Earth. Love of self and of others was lost to fear. Survival meant all had to fend for themselves and the hell with everyone else.

Many blamed their God believing they were being punished for their sins, but that was not true at all. God is love. God did not punish. Earthlings had done that to themselves. The elected officials who removed laws and protections, allowed companies to pollute in the name of putting people to work. It did not matter to them that they were the cause of the illness and death. All that mattered to them was enriching their bank accounts. The wealthy wanted more regardless of the cost to humankind.

It didn't take long for life-sustaining necessities to become toxic and dangerous for everyone. Those in power instilled violence and racism among all who walked the earth. People were labeled and put into categories based on their race, religion, color, sex, wealth, and social status. Blacks were violent. Muslims were terrorists. Females were inferior and to be treated as sex objects—it went on and on. The citizens of the United States were no longer part of one nation under God. All people are created equal was spoken but not believed or practiced.

Wealthy white males were safe if they toed the line. However, if they had love in their hearts and wanted to treat everyone with respect, they were labeled antiestablishment and subject to open ridicule. A Hitler-type society run by a dictator was feeding people false information and blaming the news media as the spreaders of fake news. The future was bleak. Earth was dying and taking all its inhabitants with it.

The wealthy 10 percent of the population and their families could invent and install personal water purification plants in their homes. They purified their air. They didn't seem to care that Earth was dying. They built bomb shelters in their homes and turned them into fortresses behind huge walls. They had guns and surveillance equipment. They had plenty of money to help them sustain their own lives. They just didn't care what happened to the other 90 percent. Greed blinded them. They did not believe there would come a time when all the money in the world would not help them survive on this dead planet. They wanted more and more. They were so busy enriching their pocketbooks. They didn't think twice about what their greed was doing to their souls.

The wealthy professed to be religious, but that was a ruse. They did not follow any of the Ten Commandments. They did not love God. They did not love each other. They cheated on their wives. They stole from the hardworking people, and they were killing them by not providing them the necessities. Yet they would go to church for the sake of appearances. They were hypocrites.

The Vatican crumbled from within as long-held secrets were revealed. The Antichrist was hard at work. Greed and power had overtaken the fabric of the men of the cloth. Faith in the Creator was lost. Those who were not wealthy and worked for a living believed their gods had forsaken them. Were all the gods deaf to the pleadings of the earthbound? Was all hope lost? Could anyone restore faith and love among the people and save the resources of Earth?

It would not be easy. It would take someone special, someone sent by the Creator who had a band of angels for protection. How could the loving souls on Earth be saved? And who could save them?

To answer these questions, one had to travel back in time to get the answer. Saving the loving souls would be a daunting task. The Creator had a plan and would have to select the right souls for the job. The timing had to be precise. There was no room for error. Come along on this magical journey that will culminate in triumph against all odds, and result in the rebirth and salvation of planet Earth.

Earth will become a planet beyond your wildest dreams where all live in peace and harmony with love in their hearts.

PART I

Life on Earth

CHAPTER 1

The Light—A Journey back Home Featuring Archangel Michael

It was a perfect day. Not a wisp of a cloud marred the bright-blue sky. The temperature was just right. The humidity was low. Palm trees hardly waved their graceful branches. The rustle of the tree leaves was not to be heard.

It doesn't get any better than this, Angie thought. Her silver Mustang had been washed inside and out, polished, gassed up, and recently serviced. She sent up her request to Archangel Michael to protect her and all those around her, and she was off cruising down the highway.

She was very glad she had gotten an early start on her trip to the Florida Keys. She would get to spend a longer day with her friends while avoiding heavy traffic. Her music was cranked up, and she was singing along to her favorite playlist. She planned to enjoy a Sunday with no work; there was nothing on her to-do list that couldn't wait. Her sons were with their families doing their own thing. She needed this chill time. After all, Sunday was a day of rest, and she planned to do just that with no guilt. Everything was right in her little corner of the world.

Bam! A loud noise shook Angie back to reality. *What was that? Did someone shoot at me? Did I hit something? Did my tire blow out? Please God, let me get over to the side of the road. I can't steer. Oh, no!*

Her beautiful Mustang was flipping over. She was dizzy—tumbling, tumbling. She felt like a rag doll in a clothes dryer. She

3

saw tree trunks quickly approaching and wondered if the trees would slow her down. *Oh God! Please help me!* She couldn't turn away from tree that stood steadfast in her path. *Archangel Michael, please help me! I'm going to hit it!*

The sound of crushing metal was followed by an eerie silence. A stillness fell over the earth. There were no sounds of vehicles, no people talking, no birds chirping—total silence. The loud crash must have scared the voices out of the woodland creatures and birds. Angie realized she didn't feel dizzy any more. She couldn't remember being hurt in the crash. She didn't feel any pain. She couldn't feel anything. She was in a state of nothingness.

As Angie lay there crumpled up in her vehicle, she started to recollect. She had been driving without a care in the world, and then she recalled that her world had literally turned upside down. Her recollection was followed by panic. *What just happened? Oh my God! I'm stuck! I can't get out! Wait! I am out of that wreck, but I can still see my crumpled body down there in the car. This doesn't seem real. It must be a dream!*

The big, puffy airbag was hiding most of her body. There was a leg where her arm should have been. Her head was flopped over next to the airbag. She heard sirens in the distance that were getting louder. *How did they find out about the accident so fast? Another motorist must have called them.* She watched the emergency responders race toward her lifeless body with fire hoses and a stretcher.

Relief flooded over her. *Fantastic. They're here. They'll help me make sense of this.*

The ear-piercing whir of the jaws of life cutting into her car was welcoming. Soon, she would be set free. But as they removed her body, she wondered, *How could I be down there and up here? I look so horrible and banged up, but I can't feel a thing.*

No one looked up. No one saw her. "Why don't you look? I'm okay! I'm up here!" she yelled, but no one heard her. Her mangled body should have been screaming with pain, but she felt quite well, better than she had a few minutes before the accident when she thought everything was perfect and wonderful. *Why didn't Archangel Michael answer my request to protect me and all those around me?* she asked herself.

Angie heard his answer in her mind. "I did protect you. I made sure you left your body before you experienced pain, and I did make sure no one was around you. It was your time."

"My time?" Angie wondered. "My time for what?"

She didn't get an answer that time. Instead, she saw.

CHAPTER 2

The Light—Crossing Over Featuring Guardian Angels Arla, Reena, and Ed

The light, the light! What is that brilliant light? Angie felt a calm come over her as she floated peacefully. She was having wonderful visions of her parents, relatives, friends, and even her pets who had passed before her. She wanted to call out to them, but she had no voice. The visions had come alive. They were extending hands to her and pointing the way toward the light, a beautiful beckoning light.

The light! She remembered the light. It was like a sunny day with the warmth of the sun beckoning. She didn't have to squint or shield her eyes. The light was drawing her closer. She felt she might be going home and started to feel giddy with excitement. *Giddy?* She wasn't one to get giddy. But giddy she felt—and happy and excited. She wondered if this was what weightlessness felt like to astronauts. The tiresome burden of listening and speaking and carefully choosing her words evaporated into the stillness and calm that enveloped her. Communication was effortless. Her thoughts were no longer of worry, fear, or concern. They were pleasant and loving, very loving.

It finally dawned on her—she was definitely going home, going back to where it had all started. She couldn't remember where she was going or where she had been, but she had a reassuring feeling that she was headed in the right direction—toward the light. She longed to reach the light. She wanted to hurry. She had a yearning to be enveloped by the brilliant, welcoming light like wrapping herself in a comfy afghan. She knew she would get there eventually. She just knew it was very good to be returning to the light, a place full of peace and boundless, unconditional love. She didn't know why she knew that, but she did.

Her mind started to adjust just as she reached the light. Love was everywhere—love, love and more love. There was so much love all around her as far as she could see and feel. She realized that her guardian angels were with her as they had been on Earth. She hadn't recognized them on Earth, but she always felt someone was watching over her and helping her. Now she knew without a doubt that they were her guardian angels, and she knew their names— Arla, Reena and Ed. *Ed*? That didn't sound right. It was such a common name, a nickname at that. *That can't be right.* But Ed let her know he did indeed have a very special name but it was difficult to pronounce and spell, so he was happy to be referred to as Ed.

It dawned on Angie that she was not speaking with a voice but communicating through her thoughts. Her guardian angels understood exactly what she was thinking, and she understood their explanations. The intensity of the love that encircled her was euphoric. She didn't care they could read her mind. She was glad she no longer had to hide what she was thinking. She knew her loving thoughts could not hurt anyone. Freedom of speech had been replaced with freedom of thought, and all she had were loving thoughts.

"Oh no!" she cried out as she found herself being pulled back away from the light. "I don't want to go back. I want to stay!"

Arla said, "You need to have closure from your visit to the earthly plane. Witnessing the end of your journey on Earth will help you transition to the spirit plane. Closure means you'll have to spend less time in the resting plane."

Angie had no idea what that meant, but she agreed to do whatever she needed to get back to the light. In an instant, she was back hovering over her mangled car. The realization of what had happened took hold of her thoughts. She had been in an accident. Her car had hit a tree. The paramedics were using the jaws of life. There were no other cars around. She thanked the Lord that no one else had been hurt. She wondered what had happened. *Did someone run me off the road and leave the scene?*

Her guardian angels brought her closer. She saw her lifeless body being pulled from the wreckage. She heard earthly voices. They were mentioning a tire-tread separation. She was surprised. There was nothing wrong with her tires. She had had them checked regularly.

"Do not place blame on yourself or anyone else. This was part of your own carefully designed plan. Your time on Earth was to end quickly. No one else was to be hurt," Arla said. "By departing in this way, attention would be drawn to the tire defect and others would be saved."

Angie worried that her family and friends would be devastated. She wanted to let them know she was safe and not to worry. Arla read her thoughts.

"You will have that opportunity, Angie, but first things first. You must stay with your earthly body until your earthbound souls have had a chance to say their goodbyes."

Angie almost panicked as she saw her body lying flat and lifeless on the gurney in the morgue. Her family was there. She wanted to let them know she was fine. Arla again reminded her that she would have that opportunity.

Time moved forward rapidly, and she found herself floating above a church service. She soon realized it was for her. Her family and friends were there. Everyone was sad, sobbing, and crying. She didn't want to see them like that. She heard them saying nice things about her, and sometimes, they would laugh as tears welled up in their eyes. The laughter filled Angie with love. She was loved, and she loved them. She hoped the sadness would leave them soon. Again, Arla read her thoughts. "It will, Angie. Time heals earthbound souls. There is no time, no clocks, no deadlines where you are going. You will see them all someday when it is their time to cross over. This is your time. Let's go back to the light."

Angie heard Arla's thoughts loud and clear, and she knew she was ready.

CHAPTER 3

Before You Go—Signs Received Featuring Archangel Azrael

She was back on the path to the light, which was beckoning her. She felt as if she were on an elevator gliding up. That time, she knew she could not be pulled back. She knew she was ascending into heaven. *Is this how Jesus and Mary felt when they ascended?*

She expected to see the pearly gates with Archangel Michael standing there in judgment. After all, that was what she had been taught in religion classes. Instead, she saw twinkling, bright-white lights like Christmas tree lights coming toward her. As the lights drew closer, a beautiful angel adorned in creamy white appeared before her with a halo with twinkling lights. Angie was not afraid. Love emanated from every part of him. His wings were enormous and strong. Before she realized what was happening, the wings encircled her in a warm, calming embrace, the most welcoming, comforting embrace she could remember.

"Welcome!" Azrael said in his commanding yet welcoming tone. "I am here to help you cross into the light."

Angie recalled that Azrael was known as the archangel of death; that conjured up images of being snatched from the comfort of Earth and hustled off to the hereafter. *How could this loving angel be the angel of death?* She forgot he could read her thoughts.

"I am the angel of death, Angie, but in a most loving way. I prefer to be called a grief counselor. I help departed souls cross over to heaven. I comfort them from the shock of leaving their earthly bodies. It is my task and pleasure to help the recently departed bring

9

closure to those they have left behind. I bring them loving comfort as they transition from the human body to the spirit body. In time, you will remember me. We have met many times before."

Angie started to recall that she did know him, but her memory was fuzzy. Maybe that is why she did not cower in the presence of this larger-than-life angel who towered over her. How could she be afraid of this archangel who emanated pure love and peacefulness?

Suddenly, her memory became crystal clear. She remembered Azrael. She had not seen or communicated with him for over a lifetime and was elated to be in his presence again. He was so strong, welcoming, and sympathetic. She loved Christmas and twinkling Christmas lights. She could never call him the angel of death. She did not even like to call him a grief counselor though that did describe his assignment. She decided to refer to him as her Christmas angel; his halo reminded her of Christmas lights heralding Jesus's birthday. Crossing over was everyone's birthday to be born on the heavenly plane. This was Angie's birthday.

"It's fine with me if you want to think of me as your Christmas angel," Azrael said as he continued to read her thoughts. "Are you okay?"

"I'm better than okay! But I'd like to make sure my friends and family could somehow know I'm fine. I'd like to help them get through their shock and grief."

"Angie, you have completed all your mandatory earthly incarnations with excellence. You will not need to return to the earthly plane to enrich your soul or work out any personal karma in the future. However, the earth is in big trouble with a darkness that has poisoned the planet. You have been chosen for an extremely important and enormous mission. You are being asked to voluntarily return for a final visit. You will oversee a mass incarnation. Many are depending on you to save the loving souls of planet Earth. We must hurry and finalize the plan so it can be set in motion. Some of the souls who are part of the master plan must incarnate before you. It all must be timed precisely like a symphony."

Angie couldn't believe what she was hearing. "Why me? What have I done that was so special? Many others must be far more worthy. I wasn't super religious. I certainly was no saint. You must have the wrong person. Others are much more pious and qualified than me. What about the pope? What about one of the saints? What about one of the Nobel Peace Prize laureates? I lived an ordinary life."

"Angie, I love the fact that you don't believe you're better than anyone else. That's part of your charm, your loving nature. Angie, you're judging yourself by Earth's standards. Perfection is not the test. The test is love. A soul must sincerely love everyone and everything. No one is perfect except our Creator. The number of times you attend a religious ceremony and your earthly notoriety are not proof of the sincere love in your heart. You didn't desire wealth or power or any of the negatives that corrupt the soul. Many, including the famous or high-ranking religious and political figures, have karma to work out in their earthly lives.

"The archangels looked for genuine love. They looked for someone who had completed his or her life mission and purpose. They reviewed the akashic records and the tapestry of life of many souls. You will learn more about these soon. Your records are consistent, and your cord in the tapestry of life is unblemished and radiates love. Time after time, life after life, you gave unconditional love with a smile and compassion. Your love touched the souls closest to you and gave us a core group of very loving souls.

"The archangels choose wisely. They brought their selection to the Creator, who studied their findings and agreed. Your loving soul will be an example to others that they do not need to achieve or attain fame or stardom. All they must do is unconditionally love everyone and everything."

Angie was still in disbelief, *But who am I to question the archangels and the Creator?* she thought. She was always ready for a challenge, and she knew the world she had left behind was in big trouble. She had been so upset that half the country followed those in power blindly like the rats had followed the Pied Piper to their doom. Those in power did not care about the people, and that infuriated her. She hadn't been able to do much about it during her last earthly visit. If given the chance again, she would gladly fight for this very important cause. She didn't know how, but time would tell. She made her decision. She was up for the challenge and boldly stated, "I'm ready. Let's go!"

They were alone in the tunnel on the way to the golden glow of the light. Where they were communicating was a pleasant place, but the light beckoned, and Angie was ready.

Azrael said, "I'm glad to see you are ready, but first, we need to give you closure on your most recent incarnation. That will prepare you for the mandatory rest period that will allow your soul to adjust to the higher vibrations of the heavenly plane. There are many steps to help you prepare for your mission to return to the earthly plane to save the loving souls. Let's start by helping those grieving souls you left behind."

"How can I help them when they can't hear me?" Angie asked.

"Remember the Christmas scarf?"

"Oh yes!" Angie said.

"Good. We'll carefully select signs for you to give to your loved ones so they will know you're fine and with them in spirit. Before we come up with these signs, we will review signs you were given by your departed loved ones. When you meet up with them on the other side, you will be able to thank them."

Angie remembered receiving signs but hadn't given them much thought.

"The Christmas scarf was a beautiful remembrance orchestrated by your mother to let you know she was fine and with your dad. I helped your mom deliver that message. Please tell me the story."

"You already know the story, Azrael. Why would you want me to tell you it?"

"I helped your mom come up with the sign and helped her and your dad deliver it to you. That was the end of my mission. I'm curious to find out what happened next."

CHAPTER 4

Before You Go—The Christmas Scarf Featuring Archangel Azrael

"Okay. Let me see. I was very sad. There was such a huge hole in my heart from the loss of my best friend, my mom. I was the only girl and her firstborn. Our Sagittarian birthdays were just weeks apart. We even shared the same name! Everyone loved Mom, and even though she had had a long life, it was so sad to see her go.

"Her illness came on suddenly. I had less than a week to adjust to the fact that she would leave me. I was settled into the hospice wing expecting to spend the next week or so with her, but I didn't have even twenty-four hours. When she stopped breathing, it didn't occur to me that she'd passed. The nurse very gently gave me the news." Angie sighed remembering the sorrow she'd faced that day, and Azrael laid a comforting hand on her shoulder.

Angie composed herself and continued. "Amid the shock and disbelief, there was paperwork and arrangements to be made. The priest came to administer the last rites. When there was nothing else for me to do, I went home to be with my family. I knew they would all be so sad. Mom had been living with us. She was part of our family, a huge part, and she would be sorely missed. I knew my mom would be with my dad.

"They had met when they were seven. Their families attended many cultural functions during their childhoods. They married when Dad returned from the service. They were so close that after he passed, we felt his presence everywhere. Parking spaces would appear out of nowhere. We spotted his looming figure in her bedroom, and we saw the indent of his head on his pillow right next to hers. We knew he was watching over all of us."

Angie looked up at Azrael; he smiled and nodded for her to continue.

"As I drove home in my bewildered state, right before me appeared an image of my mom and dad together. The image was clear as day. What caught my attention was a red-and-green plaid scarf Mom was wearing. I knew all her clothes and accessories, but I couldn't remember seeing that scarf. I wondered if she was wishing us a Merry Christmas, which was three weeks away.

"I pulled my attention away from the scarf and focused on the real message. Mom and Dad were together. It was time for Dad to bring Mom home. They looked younger, middle aged. They were side by side. That was the reassurance I needed. I arrived home and burst through the door to tell my family that Mom had passed but reassured them she was with Dad and they were fine. I explained my vision. Did my family believe me? Did they think I had imagined it? Did they think I had gone over the deep end in my sorrow? I may never know their thoughts that day, but I do know it was very real to me."

"And now you know it was real, Angie. You didn't imagine it. It was the sign your mom and dad wanted you to have. They knew you needed the assurance that they were fine and together. They also knew you would share this sign with those who needed reassurance—your husband, sons, brothers and their families."

Azrael once again gently put his hand on Angie's shoulder as she continued.

"Over the next week, the red and green scarf continued to haunt me. I looked through Mom's scarf and accessory drawers but found nothing. There had to be some reason for the scarf, but I wondered what it could be. The answer came a week later on my birthday. It was time to put up Christmas decorations. Despite my grief, I wanted to display Mom's decorations too. I knew she would have liked that. I opened her Christmas storage box, and there on top was the red and green scarf. It wasn't a neck scarf after all. It was a table scarf on which she displayed her angel collection. My heart swelled with joy. I had the proof that I hadn't imagined the vision. My husband, sons, and brothers had all seen the Christmas angel table scarf before but never as a neck scarf. Thank you, Azrael, for helping Mom deliver such a meaningful message for all of us."

Azrael's aura of twinkling Christmas lights grew brighter with Angie's expression of gratitude. "I'm delighted to know about the impact and ripple effect it had on everyone's lives. It was beyond what your parents had hoped for."

"Even when the Christmas holiday was over, the scarf was never packed away again nor was Mom's angel collection. One of Mom's favorite angels was a winking angel with a lopsided halo. Whenever I catch sight of that angel, the wink always reminds me of Mom and the Christmas scarf."

"Angie, didn't I hear about a dream you had after your mom passed?"

Angie thought about that but not for long. She remembered what most would have thought had been just a dream. "As a very sound sleeper, I rarely remembered my dreams, but this one was so real, and it stayed with me. In my sleepy state, my mom and dad took me to see my childhood house. I remember walking through the front door and going down the hallway by the bedrooms. At the end of the hallway where the bathroom used to be was an enormous staircase going down into a great room. Mom and Dad were telling me they wanted me to see this when I suddenly woke up. Curiosity got to me, so I checked my computer and entered my childhood address. I stared at the computer screen in disbelief.

"There before my eyes was a mansion. My childhood home had been torn down, and a much larger house had been built in its place. I felt sad that my home was gone, but I soon realized that no matter what had happened to my home, the treasured memories would never change. It dawned on me that I hadn't had an ordinary dream—it had been a visit from my mom and dad. I imagined that they were together checking out their memories when they came upon our old house. They shared it with me because they knew I'd share it with my brothers. We would all have the knowledge that we can continue to communicate with them as they could with us.

"I told my brothers about the visit. I suggested they check out our old address themselves. They were all amazed. We had another reassurance that Mom and Dad were fine and together and that they could communicate with us. We had received divine messages."

Azrael confirmed that Angie's parents were fine and together and that they could communicate with all of them. "We all need to open our hearts with pure love and call out to our departed loved ones, who will come to us. It's important that we don't hold them back with excessive grief. All souls need to move on from the physical plane and into the spirit world where they will be very busy.

"When two people are named after each other, you can be sure that was mutually agreed upon before they arrived on the earthly plane. When one passes, he or she returns as a spirit guide for the other. Before they can become spirit guides, they must go through special counseling to make sure they do not interfere with free will. They also need to learn how to communicate between the two planes. They are also taught how to travel between the earthly plane and the astral plane while still being available at a moment's notice."

"I know my mom was with me all the time. I had an uncanny way of glancing at the clock at precisely 11:27 which was my mom's birthday, and when that happened, whoever was in earshot would hear me say, 'Hi, Mom. Happy birthday!' My mom had always helped me when I was composing letters or doing any type of writing. After she passed, I continued to feel her making suggestions. I constantly felt her hugs and received messages from her."

"Your mom and dad travel together, so they were both with you."

Angie had thought that might be true but didn't believe she could have been so lucky to have both her parents guiding her from above. "I want to see them!"

"Patience, my dear one. You will see them soon. Now it's time to get back to the messages. Please tell me about the sign your dad left for you."

CHAPTER 5

Before You Go—Computer Gone Wild Featuring Archangel Azrael

Angie vividly remembered the sign her dad had left her. "I didn't know you could make a machine do what you made my computer do! Dad had been diagnosed with cancer and had been given three years to live. He was in an experimental drug testing group. Unfortunately, the drug he was given didn't work. We got together as often as we could though we lived in different states, and we talked all the time on the phone and exchanged emails. He had sent fun surprise packages to my sons containing rubber snakes, spiders, and other fun gifts.

"At a family reunion during Easter toward the end of the three-year diagnosis, Dad looked great, and none of us siblings, spouses, or grandkids knew how soon he would be taken from us. We didn't realize that the three years was just about up.

"The weekend was the best. The grandkids, very close in age, enjoyed fishing and taking the rowboat out on the lake behind their home. Mom cooked up a storm with our help. Fun-loving Dad never missed a beat. Treasured memories were cemented into the scrapbooks of our minds.

"About a month later, we received a call from Mom that Dad had taken a turn for the worse. The prostate cancer had spread. His prognosis was grim. We prayed for a miracle. It was hard to accept that this loving, big, strong man would soon be gone.

"A few days before he passed, he called me to say goodbye. That was the most difficult call I have ever received. He didn't want us to come to his bedside. He wanted his young grandsons to remember him as he had been during their fun-packed Easter visit a couple of months earlier. I felt a lump in my throat. It was hard to breathe and more difficult to talk without letting Dad hear the gut-wrenching sobs welling up in me. He told me that he was proud of his princess and that if there was life after death, he would give all his children a sign.

"We said our goodbyes and hung up. My suppressed anguish surfaced. I had taken the call outside by our pool so my sons wouldn't overhear me. I cried pitifully. I begged for a miracle I knew wouldn't come.

"A few hours later, he was put in a medically induced coma. On his final day on Earth, he came out of the coma and spoke of a bright light. He told my mom about all the deceased loved ones he had seen waiting to take him home. His parents, Mom's parents, some favorite brothers, and sisters-in law had all been there beckoning him. And then he was gone."

The memory of losing her dad prompted uncontrollable sobbing. Azrael wrapped his powerful wings around her until her sobbing subsided.

"Angie, your dad loved life, people, and his family especially the family get-togethers. He spread so much joy and love to all who were fortunate to have entered his world. He successfully completed his soul's mission during his stay on Earth, and so did your mom. Tell me about the signs his children received."

"All three of my brothers received the same sign on the same night—a vivid dream in which Dad took them on a journey through their lives from their earliest memories to the present. Each one had the unique experience of being the only one with Dad and reliving memory after memory. The next morning, they called each other and soon found out they had all had the same dream.

"When they called me to ask about my dream, I was forlorn and sad to admit I might have slept through my dream. I didn't remember any dream. The thought that I had missed a cherished visit with my dad haunted me over the next month. I kept sending up silent prayers to heaven asking for Dad to come back and do it again and this time help me remember it.

"But every morning, I'd wake up with no remembrance of anything. Maybe Dad kept coming to me in the night, but I had been sleeping too soundly to recall the visit. Dad knew I was a very heavy sleeper. He used to say that I worked and played so hard that I knocked myself out at night.

"One night, a tree fell next to my bedroom window during a bad storm. The fire department came out with chain saws to cut up the tree and open the roadway. The next morning, I woke up to blinding sunlight coming through my window. I wondered where the lacy sunlight and shadows that had danced on my walls every sunny morning had gone. My sleepy mind was confused. I looked out of the window and saw a pile of wood stacked up where my tree had stood. I ran to my parents to find out what had happened, and they were amazed that I hadn't heard a thing. The chain saw had buzzed for hours, but I'd slept through that. If I hadn't heard the chain saw that night, how could I have remembered a special dream from my dad? I begged Dad to give me a sign in another way."

"Angie, your dad would never give up getting a sign to you. Please continue."

"I had my own business, and Mom was my long-distance secretary. Dad assisted and even had created a side business to complement my business. We all worked closely together. Mom and I had created many form letters. I would supply the information for her to personalize the letters, and the date would prefill whatever form letter we were using. She would email me her correspondence from her home in another state. We had developed a great working relationship even though we were three hundred and fifty miles apart.

"During my early years working, if I couldn't spell a word and couldn't find it in the dictionary, I'd call Mom, and she'd give me the first letter or two, which was all I needed to get on the right track. It was amusing when I would call her because we had the same name. I would ask for her by name, and when they asked who was calling, I would again repeat her name, which was my name too. It was fun.

"I shouldn't have been surprised when my dad found a way to give me a message using the computer and the prefilled dates. The message wasn't a typed message or spontaneous writing, which could have been rationalized as my subconscious conjuring up something based on my strong desire to receive a sign. Dad and you, Azrael, came up with an amazing sign that was hard to doubt.

"One morning while I was working on form letters, the date that prefilled was not the current date but April the fourth. That was the date I had nearly died from a ruptured appendix that had burst a week prior. Dad kept asking the doctor if it was my appendix but was assured it wasn't.

"When my temperature went over a hundred and four, the on-call doctor came to my house and wouldn't even wait for an ambulance. He wrapped me in my mom's heavy winter coat, laid me in the back seat of his car, and rushed me to the hospital. They did exploratory surgery the night of April the fourth. The surgeon said I had staph, strep, gangrene, and peritonitis. I was at death's door.

"After two months in the hospital and some near-death experiences I don't remember, I was released. April the fourth became a celebration of life for my parents, my brothers, and me. How strange that this date was prefilling on my forms that day. All day, I had to back out that date and insert the correct date, but I was elated believing that that may have been my sign from my dad.

"Much to my surprise, my dad wasn't done. The next day, the date on my computer kept prefilling with his birthday. I had no doubt that was another sign. I expected it to be the final sign, a confirmation sign that my dad was sending me proof there was life after death as he had promised during the goodbye call at the swimming pool.

"But once again, Dad wasn't done. On the third day, the date that prefilled was unknown to me. It was a date before I was born. I called my mom and asked her if she knew what that date meant. Without hesitation, she told me that was the date that my dad had gone into the service. My mom knew about the prefilled dates of the past two days and understood it was her special sign.

"On the fourth day, the computer returned to prefilling the current date. What an amazing sign to have received. It was unbelievable! No one believed me when I told them about it, but I didn't care. The signs were for me, and I had received them loud and clear—my dad was fine."

CHAPTER 6

Before You Go—Visitations Featuring Archangel Azrael

Azrael's aura got brighter. "Yes, Angie, we can do many things. We can make phones ring. We worked very hard to get a sign to you, and we didn't give up until you had received it. Your dad had made a promise to his princess that he was determined to keep, and he did. Tell me about the sign your grandfather gave you after he passed."

"Azrael, that was the first sign I ever received. I was thirteen and had been lying on my bed reading when I looked up and saw my grandfather, whom we called Papa, sitting on my comfy, tufted chair in the corner of my room. He looked so real. I got up and went to him, but just then, my mom called my brothers and me downstairs. I instinctively turned to her voice, and when I looked back, Papa had vanished.

"I hurried downstairs. Mom asked us to sit at the dining room table. She said that Papa, who had been in the hospital, had just passed away. I was shocked. I remember wondering if he had come to me to say goodbye. I couldn't tell anyone what I had experienced. They would never have believed me.

"Many years later when my mom started seeing visions of my dear departed dad, I told her how Papa had visited me on the day she had told us he had passed. Mom believed me and was comforted to know her father had given us a sign that he was fine."

"Yes, Angie. He wanted you to know he was thinking of you. Your mom, dad, and grandfather picked out special signs for you. It's almost time for us to come up with some signs for the loved ones you have left behind. But first, tell me about your sign from your special Uncle Jim."

The golden light of the tunnel continued to envelop them. However, the light at the end of the tunnel was still beckoning her.

"Uncle Jim lived in California. He was a retired navy chaplain and was very dear to my husband and me. He knew how much we wanted to adopt a child. We had so much love to give and wanted to share it. Uncle Jim understood and agreed to pray for us. We knew his prayers had been answered when our first son was born on Uncle Jim's birthday. We enjoyed many visits over the years. And then one day, he was gone. Jim appeared to have died peacefully in his sleep. My husband had gone across country to handle the funeral arrangements and pay our respects while I stayed home with our sons.

"While the estate was being processed through the courts, my husband was in a car accident and was unable to make the return trip to California to finalize the estate. I made the trip on his behalf. My mom stayed with my husband to help him while he was in a halo cast. I dropped off our sons at the airport to go to Canada to a hockey tournament with another hockey family. I boarded a plane for the long trek across county."

"Angie, I know how hard it was for you to leave your sons in the care of others and leave your husband at a time when he needed you. But you put your trust in the Lord and went on to complete the task that had been thrust on you."

"And that task was huge. I didn't know how I could take care of the house, possessions, vehicle, banking, and so much more in one week, but I knew I had to try. The three-hour time difference and need to get things done quickly motivated me to work right through that first night.

"In the morning, I needed something to eat, gas for the car, and a place to drop off his used clothes. Two blocks from his house, I saw a gas station with a breakfast wagon and a Goodwill truck in the parking lot. How fortunate was that? From that day on, everything fell into place. I knew that Uncle Jim, my dad, and my father-in-law were all with me. I told them that I didn't need their help when I took a shower as I shut the door. I cleaned the house, went through all the contents, held a garage sale, got the house listed, groomed the yard, and sold the car in one week. What I accomplished had not been humanly possible.

"I knew I had received incredible divine assistance one day when I forgot to turn on the garage light so I could read the car's speedometer. The garage door opened by itself. I walked back into the kitchen and remembered that I had forgotten to close the garage door, but it had closed by itself. No way that could have happened on its own. That was my sign that they were there helping me. I was too busy to grieve, but why should I have grieved anyway while they were there with me?"

"Yes, Angie, they were there with you. You were willing to help them, so they felt the least they could do was help you and let you know they there. That's why they arranged for the Goodwill truck and the lunch wagon to be at the gas station right when you needed them and why they opened and closed the garage door."

"I'm so happy to know my suspicions are confirmed, Azrael! They had been there! Despite my busy schedule, I had a couple of pleasant memories to treasure from my trip. I was driving on the freeway and saw the most incredible array of colors in a field of wildflowers. It was beautiful. I had never seen them before on any of our previous visits. That memory is engraved in my mind.

"When I was driving to the church where Uncle Jim said Mass to drop off his priestly garments, I turned a corner and there was a mountain right in front of me. At that same moment, a song by the rock group Yes was playing on the radio. They were my favorite group. The verse they were singing was 'Mountains come out of the sky and they stand there.' That mountain was right in front of me. That line in that song brings me back to that very mountain every time I hear it."

"Yes, Angie, they wanted to give you some happy memories. We can nudge a radio station disk jockey to play a certain song at a certain time. We also helped you coordinate the care of your injured husband and young sons to free you up to make the journey across country. They watched after you all the time as your spirit guides. They watched over your family too. Your departed loved ones have always been there for you just as your guardian angels and the archangels are always there for the asking. You will see them all soon."

It dawned on Angie that her husband might have been in that accident so she would have to go to California in his place. For a moment, she was nearly paralyzed with fear at the thought she might have been the cause of her husband's harm.

Azrael quickly calmed her fears. "Don't worry, Angie. You and your husband had made these plans long before you were incarnated. The accident was something he needed to endure to enrich his soul. Everyone must experience all emotions including pain. You had agreed to this beforehand."

Angie gave a sigh of relief.

CHAPTER 7

Before You Go—Signs Given Featuring Archangel Azrael

"Angie, it's time to come up with the perfect signs for you to give your loved ones and special friends. Please tell me about your sons. They were a huge part of your life. Some of the challenges you and your husband faced were planned before you incarnated on the earthly plane, but you wouldn't have realized that at the time."

Angie thought about her grown sons who were so special to her. She understood that by recalling their story, it would help her select perfect signs for them to remember her by, signs that would let them know she was fine and still close by.

"The story of my sons began when I was fifteen and my appendix ruptured a week before I was operated on. I spent two months in the hospital and endured several operations and many setbacks. So many people prayed for me. I was included in many prayer chains. Those prayers along with my determination helped me pull through. The doctors told me I'd probably never be able to have children, but that didn't matter; I had survived. Having children was very far from my mind at that young age.

"However, when I met the love of my life, it was very much on my mind. It was only fair that he knew. When we starting talking about marriage, I told him I could not have children. That's when he told me he was adopted. We realized it was part of God's plan that we were destined to be adoptive parents."

"Angie, it was not only God's plan for you and your husband to be adoptive parents. You now realize it was part of your souls' plan with the blessing of all the angels and the Creator."

"I'm starting to understand that all souls map out plans for their journeys on the earthly plane before they get here."

"Angie, all souls formulate plans to work out their karma before they arrive on the earthly plane. Say for instance someone had been cruel. That person might decide to return as the recipient of cruelty to understand and to clear that negative karma. Regardless of the best intentions made ahead of time, all souls go through the veil of forgetfulness. They don't remember any details of the plan when they arrive. They also have free will to make choices. Sometimes, they make wrong choices and go down a different path. Choices can alter the soul's plan. When the soul returns to the astral plane, the life's path is reviewed. Maybe the soul will want to return to work out the same or new karma. The Creator along with the archangels knows how a soul's plan interacts with the plans of other souls. Everything must be synchronized."

"Thank you, Azrael. I understand that better. I'll continue with the story of my sons. After we were married, we applied to many adoption agencies. No conditions—we just wanted a child or children to love. We didn't care what color, religion, or age they were. We agreed to take an older sibling group. It was disheartening to learn that children in the foster-care system were stuck there because you guessed it—money. Foster parents make money taking care of foster children. Some state employees earn a salary taking care of foster children. Once those children are adopted, those depending on that income suffer. It didn't seem to matter that the real victims were the children. My husband and I helped get new laws enacted to help free children from the foster-care system and into permanent and loving homes. Meanwhile, we remained childless and waiting.

"Ten years later, we were on vacation visiting Uncle Jim in California. He had a comfortable house north of San Diego. He was such a personable guy and such fun. He understood how much we wanted children and said he would pray for us."

"Angie, your Uncle Jim was a very special soul. He touched so many lives as a chaplain on aircraft carriers and when he worked at churches on the mainland. You and your husband saw only a small portion of the positive impact he had on others."

"Wow!" Angie exclaimed. "I had no idea, but I'm not surprised. Everyone loved Uncle Jim. Shortly after our visit with him, my husband showed me a newspaper article about Korean adoptions. We carefully considered the foreign-adoption option. After ten years, there was no progress on the American adoption waiting lists. Abortions were an accepted practice, and there were not enough children released from foster care to meet the demand. We wanted children, and the foreign-adoption opportunity was practically handed to us.

"There was a ton of paperwork, but we submitted our application. We had to clear background checks for two governments and be fingerprinted. Everyone we knew had been praying for us. We had far more references than we needed, but we sent them all in for good measure. Finally, all requirements were submitted, all interviews were completed, and we were officially on the Korean adoption waiting list. We wondered how long that would take.

"We were pleasantly surprised. Seven months after our California visit with Uncle Jim, we received a call that they had a boy for us. We were elated. And imagine our surprise when we learned our son had been born on Uncle Jim's birthday. It was a sign from heaven. His prayers had been answered, and so had ours. We soon had our first son, and we named him after Uncle Jim.

"Two and a half years later, we were blessed with our second son. The call from the adoption agency came on St. Paddy's day, so we named him Patrick. Our sons were a delight from the moment they were put in our arms. They knew I believed in life after death, so I need to come up with a sign that they'll know is from me."

"And that we will do," Azrael said. "They know about your keen belief in angels. They know you inherited your mom's angel collection and have added to it. They know you were always calling on the angels for assistance and guidance, and you had taught them which archangel to call on in every situation. They heard you thank the angels."

Patty Callahan

"I need to send my sons a sign that I am with my angels. I could send them feathers as in angel feathers. At one time, I had nine birds. I still have some of their feathers in my office. Would the feathers make them think of my pet birds instead of angels? I'd love to appear to them in their dreams just as my father did with my brothers. Or in an image like my parents gave me. They could have the same dream or vision on the same night of me surrounded by my beloved angels. They would wake and share their mutual dream and recognize it as a sign. Then I could leave them feathers as a sign that would continue over time.

"Perhaps pennies would be better than feathers. I had helped them monetarily and had taken care of the household finances. They had very seriously saved for their own homes. They would understand the sign of pennies ... or would they? But pennies from heaven doesn't mean I'm with my angels."

"Angie, it sounds like you've made your decision. The most meaningful sign would be angels. They know that the only item you couldn't resist when you went shopping was angels. You had angel earrings and angel pins. Your Christmas tree was adorned with angels of every type and size. You found angel wind chimes and angel bookmarks. You read every book you could find on angels. You should give them angels as their sign. They might see an angel while they were out shopping or see angels in a magazine or on a billboard. Every time they see an angel, they'll think of you. This will be a lifetime remembrance for them to have. How does that sound?"

"That's perfect! Let's do it!"

"Consider it done, Angie."

Azrael asked about Angie's friends.

"I want each sign to be meaningful for them, Azrael, so this will be more difficult and time consuming. I'm starting to get anxious. I want to move on in my journey to the light. I want to see the other archangels, and I hope to see my husband, my kindred spirit."

Azrael reminded her that it seemed she already knew what sign to leave. "Why are you making this so difficult? Leave them angel signs as well. They'll know you are fine but also that angels exist and help is there for the asking."

"Yes!" Angie exclaimed. "Angel signs for everyone! Angel signs sent from above with love and angel blessings!"

"Since everyone knows your fondness for angels, they'll think of you every time they see an angel. Hopefully, this will remind them to talk to their angels."

Angie and Azrael were happy. It was time to move toward the light, the beacon of love and peace.

PART II

Life in the Spirit Realm

CHAPTER 8

Homeward Bound—Through the Light Featuring Archangel Jeremiel

Azrael bid Angie farewell. "You have done very well in closing the chapter on this incarnation. Now it's time for me to say goodbye to you, my dear one, and attend to those who are grieving at your loss. It's time to ask Jeremiel to bring you through the light."

Azrael faded into the distance. Another beautiful archangel appeared before her. He towered over Angie but did not frighten her. He was adorned in dark purple with golden lights sparkling around his head like a halo. The gold sparkles reminded Angie of gold gems reflecting light in all directions like shooting stars. It was a beautiful sight. Angie would think of Jeremiel as her golden star angel. That would help her remember him because at that time, he did not seem familiar to her. She struggled to remember him. He wrapped his wings around her in a loving embrace that gave her a feeling of peacefulness and the realization that it did not matter whether she could remember him at that moment; she knew she would in time.

"I am Jeremiel, the archangel of hope. I come to you with peace and love. My mission is to present recently departed souls with divine visions to prepare them for the spirit plane and to minister to the souls who are ready to ascend to heaven. Come, my child. It's time to go through the light and leave the veil of forgetfulness behind you. Everything will be revealed shortly. You have a great mission before you, but first, you will visit with your departed loved ones followed by your rest period. Then the planning for your future and the future of humanity will begin."

"I'm ready!" Angie said. "Let's go!"

Angie saw the light ahead of her, and as she traveled up, she saw her life flash before her.

"Don't be startled, my dear child of God. You must see the life you are leaving behind through the eyes of love, not the critical, judgmental eyes of others or even yourself. Fear not. You lived an exemplary life and have fulfilled all the plans you had hoped to accomplish on this, your last mandatory earthly visit in human form. You will have another chance to review your life later. There will be plenty of time for analysis, but as one of a higher vibration than you have, I say rest assured that you will be happy with your own results. Right now, we are imprinting these images and memories in your soul for your karma. These details will be available to you and for everyone to review and refer to."

She was seeing something like a digital photo album set at warp speed. Image after image flew by; she could barely keep up. She saw her parents, siblings, relatives, friends, husband, children, in-laws, and work acquaintances flash before her eyes. The memories were solidifying their place in her soul. A wave of relief washed over her. She was seeing her life through loving eyes. Memories and knowledge came flooding back to her.

"Angie, the memories of your experiences during this earthly incarnation are being cataloged in your soul's knowledge base. The information will be available to be viewed and shared by everyone including yourself. Some may want to see and experience one aspect of your earthly life while others may want to watch the entire journey of your soul. Many will learn from reviewing your experiences on the spirit side as you learned from your experiences on the earth's side. Since you have been chosen to lead a mass incarnation to save the loving souls of the world, the souls who will incarnate with you may want to understand every aspect of your soul to ensure they can work with you in harmony. Undoubtedly, you will also want to study them."

Jeremiel led the way toward the beautiful light beckoning to Angie. It seemed brighter than the sun, but it did not hurt her eyes.

She felt she was traveling in a regular earthly express elevator without any walls, floor, or ceiling, but it did not frightener her.

As they broke through the light, she felt exhilarated. She felt the silver cord that bound her to life on Earth disappear. She knew that once that cord was cut, she could not go back. She would be able to visit only in spirit form, but that didn't bother her. She was filled with a love, peace, and joy far beyond any she remembered or had ever felt on Earth. She was ready for whatever came next. She had no fear though she did not have any remembrance of being there before. *Not yet anyway*, she thought. She felt she would understand in time.

Angie saw those who had passed before her reaching out and encouraging her to come to them. She saw her dear, sweet mother; the hard worker everyone had loved and called Mom. Angie always felt so fortunate to have had her as her earthly mom. And there was her dad, who had taught his princess so much including loving, caring principles to live by. And there were her husband's parents. They had welcomed her into their family and had been so kind to her, her parents, and her children.

Her last memories of both sets of parents included illness and death. She was elated to see that they all looked years younger, healthy, and happy. She seemed to know but could not remember another couple standing with them. She looked around and saw her cousins, aunts, uncles, and friends welcoming her as if to a big party, a reunion of sorts. There were hugs galore. Love was in the air. She loved them all, and they loved her unconditionally.

There was a ruckus. She turned to see what was going on. She saw spots—spots in the form of her graceful, energetic Dalmatians romping over to greet her—Bosco, Patches, Junior, and Wendy looked happy and healthy and ready to play. Angie had had no idea her pets would be waiting for her in heaven. And there was her husband's childhood Lab, Sinbad. Her pet birds fluttered around her head. Her canaries, parakeets, cockatiels, and parrot were all trying to land on her. She stretched out her arms, and they took up their places tweeting and singing. The music delighted her soul. She was amazed at how all her pets got along so well, but after all, it was heaven, a place where love filled the air. There was no dominance or jealousy. There were fields for the dogs to run and trees for the birds. Angie encouraged her pets to enjoy it all; she would see them later.

Angie could hardly contain her excitement as she exclaimed, "What a glorious place!"

CHAPTER 9

Homeward Bound—The Reunion Featuring Archangel Jeremiel

As her jubilation became manageable, she became conscious of the fragrance of flowers. She smelled the sweet perfume of the roses, the strong aroma of springtime jasmine, and the subtle but undeniable fragrance of lilacs. The memorable scent of the gardenias reminded her of her wedding bouquet and the six-foot-tall bush that bloomed outside her bedroom window.

She marveled at how she smelled the flowers individually and yet at the same time. They did not overpower each other; each distinct, sweet smell tickled her senses and brought with it a cherished memory. Fields of poppies rivaled those from one of her favorite movies. Stately trees in the distance were showing off their canopies of lush, green leaves. The colors were more vivid and clearer than she had witnessed on Earth; it was as if she had put on a new pair of glasses and could see even the veins on the leaves. The gardens were immaculate. There were no weeds to pull, no dead flowers to trim, no leaves to rake—no upkeep needed, no effort required. Everywhere she looked was another beautiful vision. It was indeed Paradise.

As her senses of sight and smell settled down, she realized she was in a gorgeous field teeming with flowers. She saw her dad admiring some beautiful deep-red, bright-red, pink, and yellow roses. Their petals looked like velvet. He looked so content in his rose garden. Then she noticed her mother-in-law surrounded by her favorite pale-violet lilacs. The hydrangea bushes were teeming with multicolored blooms the size of dinner plates that bounced around like pom-poms.

An entire fence was full of every color of morning glory imaginable. Her mother-in-law looked so happy among her favorite flowers—canna lilies, tiger lilies, caladiums, gladiolas, geraniums, marigolds, zinnias, alyssum, snapdragons, and more all exquisitely adorned in their colorful dresses. She saw her mom admiring them and hanging baskets overflowing with gorgeous blooms creating a brilliantly colored palette. These were all her mom's favorites, and she looked so happy touching and smelling them. Amid the delightful fragrances of all the flowers, Angie caught a whiff of her mom's favorite perfume.

A babbling brook only a foot deep and about ten feet wide ran through the field. It was just like her beloved Jenny Jump State Park. She saw it as she remembered it from her youth and before they had dammed it up for an amusement park. Frolicking in the water's edge were unicorns. She blinked. Yes—beautiful, mystical, magical unicorns.

Jeremiel spoke. "Unicorns had been part of the animal kingdom on Earth. Poachers killed them for their horns to the point of extinction. Now, they roam freely here with no fear."

She could not have imagined anything more wonderful, happy, beautiful, and peaceful. Happiness coursed through her.

She caught a glimpse of her beloved husband, Andrew, off to the side and patiently waiting his turn. She could no longer contain herself. She rushed to him, and their spirits united. Feelings of pure love, devotion, elation, and bliss engulfed them. They were together again. And together, they would incarnate and save the world. They would be unstoppable.

Angie had been heartbroken when he passed before she did, but she always felt his presence. It didn't matter she couldn't see him. She had spoken to him and knew he had heard her. She had worked out all decisions with him. Sometimes, he had helped her think things through, and she would come up with better options. She was certain he had whispered those thoughts to her.

She always felt that his affirmations gave her the confidence to move on with life on Earth without him. When grief had overwhelmed her and the hole in her heart seemed too big to heal, she felt his warm embrace while soothing thoughts flooded her. Their love was everlasting; they were together again. It became clear to her that he had to return first to start planning the mass incarnation; it was necessary and part of the plan.

"I never left your side on Earth," he said. "You often visited me on the spirit plane during some of your dream times. I know that you rarely remember your dreams, so I don't expect you to remember those visits. During the times you missed me most, I made sure you came to me in the spirit world. I missed you so much and had to let you know we were never apart. I love you, Angie, and always will."

Angie hugged him. "Andrew, I always felt your love. I remember the mornings I hated to wake up. Those were probably the mornings after we had spent the evening together. Those were the times I didn't want to end. I'm thrilled we're together again. I feel I'm going to burst!"

"Being together during dream times helped us endure the days without each other," he said. "Our nights together were spent working on the future incarnation. We accomplished a lot during those meetings, and as soon as you complete your resting phase, we'll review the plans together."

Angie realized what he was telling her was true; it was as if she were recovering from amnesia; her memories slowly returned.

Jeremiel, who had been waiting nearby, said, "Angie, you'll remember everything when the time is right. Remembering every detail all at once can be overwhelming."

Angie understood; she decided she would be patient. Jeremiel stepped back; he gave her time to be greeted by her huge fan club. Angie noticed that he was smiling while he watched her. In due time, he said, "Angie, it's time for your resting stage."

"I feel fine! Can't I skip that part? I want to stay for a while longer. Please. I didn't get a chance to talk to everybody."

"Angie, I'm often asked that. You know you cannot, but you will come back. You must not skip the resting stage. It's a necessary part of your transition from earthbound soul to higher-vibrational soul. Your stay in the resting stage will be minimal, so let's get started. After you awaken from your rest, you will come back for a longer visit, and everyone will be waiting for you. They are planning a banquet in your honor.

"You have a huge mission ahead of you, and there's no time to waste. I don't mean time in the sense of the spiritual plane where time doesn't exist. I'm referring to time on the earthly plane, and the time for you to make your reentry is rapidly approaching. Many of your friends will make the trip with you as part of the mass incarnation. They know the importance of the resting phase."

Reluctantly but knowingly, Angie resigned herself to go with Jeremiel while the others vowed they would see her again soon.

CHAPTER 10

Time to Rest Featuring Archangel Jeremiel

Jeremiel whisked Angie away from the beauty of the land with all its flowers and delightful fragrances and the sounds of wind chimes on the gentle breezes. Her loving husband, pets, dear friends, family— her kindred souls—were left behind.

She was in what appeared to be a hospital. It was very quiet but bustling in stark plainness compared to where she had just been. Nurses who seemed to be angels glided through the hallways appearing and then vanishing before her eyes. Angie and Jeremiel nodded to those they passed. Wards were on both sides of the enormous hallway. One wing was definitely off limits; she saw no signs to that effect, but she felt it was a "do not enter" area. Angie was concerned.

Jeremiel sensed her concern and explained matters. "This is the wing for severely damaged souls. There are murders and those who caused great harm to masses of people. They lost love in their hearts and made wrong choices with their free will. They will need to have love restored to their souls before they can appreciate being on the loving spirit plane. Their karma is severely affected, and it could take many incarnations to repair the damage they have done to their souls by harming others. They will have very long resting periods followed by therapy to rejuvenate their damaged souls. It will take time and patience."

Angie saw that the angels in that area appeared to be very serious in their efforts to minister to these souls. Most of the patients were floating in a sleep state. Others seemed combative and were challenging the nurses. Still others were deep in conversation. She could not hear them, but she sensed what was going on.

At the next ward, Jeremiel continued his explanation. "Some of these souls are fighting the transition to the spirit plane. They want to go right back to Earth because they're missing someone or missing the lives they might have abruptly left. Others do not believe they have passed on. Some are being pulled back by desperately grieving loved ones who won't let them go. These souls need counseling, sympathy, and assistance. Some will work with Archangel Azrael to send more signs to grieving loved ones to help them move on in life so they can let their departed loved ones transition."

Angie nodded. They passed another corridor and peeked into a wing with beds as far as she could see. Above each bed was a peacefully floating soul. Jeremiel said, "These souls need more rest than you do. They had not been able to accomplish everything they'd set out to accomplish in their lives. They need to learn to love themselves for what they had accomplished. They need to learn to let go of their self-imposed disappointment over their incomplete plans. Souls are their own worst critics. They need to learn there is no need for judgment from themselves or anyone else. Any unfinished business will be handled in a future incarnation. Over time, they will all transition out of the resting stage."

As they neared the end of the hospital corridor, there was one wing left. Jeremiel introduced Angie to the ward she would be staying in. "This ward is for those who require only a short resting period like you, Angie. You will be joining them shortly."

She saw many souls lying still while floating above their beds. It was a very quiet and peaceful room. None of the wards was adorned with anything because those in them were asleep and no one could visit them. Jeremiel directed Angie to one bed and seemed to gently lift her into a lying position above it. She was astonished. She never felt his hands helping her. Her body was weightless. She was comfortable and ready to drift off to sleep.

Jeremiel whispered, "Enjoy your rest, my dear one. We will meet again."

Angie sleepily asked, "Will you be here when I wake up?"

"When your soul is ready, you will awaken refreshed. I won't be here when you wake up, but we'll know, and we'll come to help you with the next phase of your reentry into the spirit world. You'll be met by an archangel who will help you get refreshed and ready for your special reunion with your family and friends."

Angie thought about those who were waiting for her, a delightful thought as she drifted off to sleep. She smiled. She could not wait to see her husband and everyone else again. She knew there was no use delaying the inevitable. The sooner she started the rest period, the quicker she would be in Andrew's arms again.

"Enjoy your slumber, Angie," Jeremiel whispered as he wrapped his powerful wings around her in a calming embrace.

She was very sleepy. The feeling reminded her of meditation when she would clear her mind and push thoughts away. She felt she was entering a hypnotic state, a trance. The last thing she remembered seeing was the golden, sparkling stars of Jeremiel's halo as he faded into the distance. Her thoughts and memories vanished into thin air. She was no longer aware of anything. The resting phase had begun. She felt herself falling into a deep slumber. She knew nothing would awaken her until she was ready.

CHAPTER 11

Awaken and Beautify Featuring Archangel Jophiel

Angie realized she was no longer in a sleep state. The faint tinkle of thousands of wind chimes filled the air. *What a wonderful sound to wake up to. Every alarm clock should be so gentle and pleasing*, she thought. The melodious sound was hypnotic. Angie heard a gentle voice that sounded like a harp. She saw a beautiful female archangel with hot-pink sparkles like glitter glistening around her head. She looked like a porcelain doll adorned in an exquisite, deep-pink gown made of a graceful fabric that flowed like a waterfall while it danced in the wind.

"I trust you enjoyed your rest. I am Archangel Jophiel. Some call me the archangel of beauty. I am here to prepare you for your return to a relaxing time with your family and friends."

Angie was excited and ready. She could not contain herself as she blurted out, "Let's go!"

"Patience, my dear. We want you to look your best, and I'm here to help you. You had a rough exit from the earthly plane and then a quick visit with your family and friends before your rest period. Your mind is clear and ready to soak in the beauty, scents, and sounds that will further beautify your soul.

"My dear one, let me ask you, when you woke up in the morning on the physical plane, did you rush out the door without refreshing yourself and selecting an outfit? Some days, it might have felt that way, but it wasn't by choice. Maybe your alarm clock didn't go off. Maybe there was no hot water. Maybe you tripped in the mud while

44

you rushed somewhere. During your resting stage, you washed away the past including the heavy pull of gravity you endured on the earthly plane. It's time to freshen up and select an outfit for the next phase of your exciting journey."

Angie found herself in a beauty parlor chair in a room bustling with activity. She was the focus of everyone's attention. She heard "Over the Rainbow" playing in the background and finally understood the lyrics. She was there and indeed over the rainbow. *The Wizard of Oz* had been her favorite movie since childhood. Her mind drifted back to when Dorothy and her friends were freshened up for their visit with the great and powerful Oz. She almost expected to see the Horse of a Different Color prance by. She brought herself back to the present and realized she felt clean; her skin was radiant and smooth. Her hair was glistening and silky, and it smelled wonderful. Her long, blond hair was full of ringlets and felt bouncy. She wondered how they had done that so fast without her realizing it. Beautiful gowns were brought forward, and her favorite was selected without her uttering a word. *How did they know I wanted that particular one?*

The one they had selected for her was yellow with a white-eyelet bodice. She felt like she had scarves gracefully flowing down from her shoulders, but they were the long sleeves that were open and wide at her wrists. The bottom of the gown was embroidered with colorful flowers. She felt as if she were tiptoeing through a flower garden. The skirt swayed gently as she walked. It was very feminine, and Angie felt graceful. The gown was elegant, but it was also comfortable and practical. She could run and skip and twirl around without worrying about ripping it.

The experience was magical. She was speechless as she watched her transformation into a beautiful, graceful angel to match her name. It was like her fairy godmother had waved her wand and Cinderella was ready for the ball. Angie did not have wings, but she did not mind or even question whether she would ever have wings.

They must have known she was not a fan of shoes. She usually wore sneakers and would kick them off in favor of bare feet whenever possible. She looked at her feet and saw sandals that molded to her feet in such a way that she could not feel them. She spun like a ballet dancer doing a pirouette. She was surprised at how wonderful she felt. It was time to make her grand entrance.

Jophiel said, "You look absolutely beautiful, a divine vision of loveliness. Angie, always remember to spend time outside and enjoy the fresh air. Be sure to connect with nature. Your mother used to bundle you up on the coldest days and place your baby carriage in the perfect place for you to soak up the rays of the sun. She was wise to do that. Fresh air, sunlight, and moonlight help relieve stress and let you develop new, creative ideas. Even infants need to have stress released from the bombardment of new information thrown at them. As infants and toddlers with minds like sponges, they must develop their own coping mechanisms to process the endless wave of facts.

"On the spirit plane, all souls must continue to release stress as they plan their futures here or when they return to the physical plane. While you're enjoying the magnificent flower gardens in the vast outdoors, you will also be enjoying your family and friends. You are ready now. It's time for me to bid you farewell. I will see you again in the spirit world and later in the physical world so I can continue to help you beautify your mind and appearance. You will need to achieve a look of feminine beauty with a strength that commands respect that will help you achieve your goals. Now it is time for you to go with Ariel."

Jophiel bowed and gracefully disappeared with her flowing gowns wafting on the gentle breezes. Angie watched the pink sparkling glitter fade as she marveled at her beauty.

CHAPTER 12

Nature's Marvels Featuring Archangel Ariel

Angie found herself standing on the edge of a field that stretched as far as she could see. Tall grasses and shocks of brilliant colors were swaying in the breeze. Butterflies of every shape and color darted around adding another level of color. Birds were calling to each other; their songs filled the air. She recognized the sounds of cardinals and blue jays. Some parrots had quite a dialogue going on. She heard the cheerful sounds of children playing in the fields and dogs barking. The sun was shining, and puffy, white clouds drifted across the blue sky. Double rainbows arched in all their splendor. She soaked up the sun and fresh air as Jophiel had said she should.

She was startled back to reality by a jovial voice that seemed to slide in on a gentle breeze. A cheerful "Hello!" blended with the sounds of nature that filled the air. Before her was a vision of loveliness befitting the surroundings. This archangel reminded her of a fairy princess dressed in a pale-pink gown and a crown shimmering with pale-pink diamonds that reflected the sunlight. The lovely archangel held two colorful bouquets. She offered one to Angie and said, "I am Ariel. I'm pleased to meet you, Angie. You look fabulous—all rested and refreshed. I am the nature angel, the archangel of the outdoors. It's my job to make sure all the gardens are tended and everyone knows that every creature from the smallest to the largest is one of God's creatures that serves a purpose and must be treated with respect.

"It is also my duty to remind everyone especially on the physical plane that the earth is God given and they must not destroy it. The planet is fragile, and I am very sad to report that it is on the verge of dying. Many souls have voluntarily returned to Earth with the enormous task of attempting to enlighten people and make them unite in their commitment to preserve their planet.

"We thought we were getting somewhere. Those in power passed laws to protect the lands. They were holding companies accountable for their actions. Serious discussions with other countries resulted in agreements about climate change. But recently, a new administration eliminated all the laws that were protecting the earth. It was so obvious to the masses that the laws were necessary. People asked why this was. The answer was simple—greed. Corporations would become richer if they didn't have to abide by the protection laws. We cannot wait four or eight more years for a new administration to reinstitute the laws that protect the lands. The earth is in a death spiral, and its demise would affect every planet in every galaxy. All the universes are in peril. But right now is your time, a joyous time. It's time to go back to the flower gardens and spend time with your family and friends who have been waiting patiently for your return."

"Will Andrew be there?" Angie asked hopefully.

"Absolutely! He is most anxious to behold his soul mate again."

In an instant, they were back in the beautiful gardens. Everything was perfect; it was the most beautiful flower show imaginable. Her beloved Andrew swept her up in his arms and twirled her around. Angie's gown gracefully encircled them in a vortex of yellow. They were remembering their wedding day and first dance and all their other dances on Earth. Their love radiated far beyond their affectionate embrace. Their combined energy was powerful beyond imagination. Angie had always known they were soul mates.

As if on their own cloud, they glided over to huge banquet. Cornucopias overflowed with vegetables of every type and color. Some were fresh and raw for the taking, and others had been prepared in delightfully fragrant dishes. She saw an abundance of every kind of juicy and perfectly ripened fruit including melons, apples, peaches, apricots, oranges, and tangerines. There were thirst-quenching, fruity beverages of all types. Everything was scrumptious. All the food was plant based. No animal would ever be harmed for human consumption on the astral plane; that would have been inconceivable. The servers were angels with gowns swaying in the breeze and sparkling halos.

Andrew helped her into her seat next to him at the head of the table; she was the honored guest. Family and friends took their places at the great banquet table. Angie could barely contain her delight. The dishes were passed, and food was sampled. Each bite assaulted the palate with a burst of delicious flavor. Stories were shared; they centered around memories of Angie. Her dad told stories of one of their many outings in her youth including those to Swartswood Lake, Bear Mountain, Albany, Florida, and Jenny Jump State Forest.

Her dad told everyone of one day that Angie had taken off from work. The family boat was towed down to the river for her private use that day. Off she went to an island accessible only by boat. She had not planned on falling asleep, but the warm sun and the gentle lapping of the waves rocked her into a deep slumber. When she woke up, she was lobster red on the front and chalky white on the back. To make matters worse, the tide had gone out and the boat was beached. It was too heavy for her to pull back into the water. She had no choice but to wait in the hot sun with no shelter until the tide came back in. She had been quite a sight until the red faded.

Her mom told stories of family gatherings and making apple fritters for everyone. She told the story of the time Angie got off from work early and decided to bake chocolate chip cookies for everyone. Her brothers came home and grabbed some. Moments later, they were spitting them into the sink. Angie retraced her steps and figured out she had added steak sauce instead of vanilla to the batter. After that, she tasted her dishes before serving them.

Angie almost giggled when she saw her dad pinch her mom's bottom. After he had passed, her mom had sworn she didn't remember him ever doing that. We all knew how she squealed when she was standing at the sink and he came up behind her and gave her a little pinch. We wondered how Mom could have forgotten one of his favorite loving gestures. Mom smiled at Angie.

Angie's loving husband, her soul mate, remained by her side as they listened. They would have a chance to privately talk among themselves later, but for the time being, they were enjoying the memories.

There was a nudge at her elbow; she turned and saw one of her favorite Dalmatians, Patches. She laughed with delight as she recalled how much Patches loved food. They had a pet name for her—Fat Dog. She had a large build, but she also loved food. Soon, Patches' son, Junior, was barging his way in at the table, so Angie decided it was time to take them to romp in the fields. Outside, the Dalmatian Wendy brought her a ball to throw. Soon, Bosco came bounding over. Andrew joined her as their pet Dalmatians retrieved the tossed balls. It was such fun to watch them as they frolicked together. Soon, it was time to return to the gathering to hear some more stories and continue their journey down memory lane.

Back inside the enormous tent, she heard her father-in-law telling how her husband's dog used to lick Angie's toes. Her mother-in-law told the story about Uncle John's dog rushing into the kitchen one time; they threw spaghetti noodles on him to calm him down. Angie saw the couple with her husband's parents again and finally remembered them. Andrew had been adopted; they were his birth parents. Birth parents send angels to watch over their children. When they pass, they return as spirit guides. Angie had always sensed there were many angels and guides around her husband, and she started recognizing them. Their incarnation plans for their past life had included her husband being adopted so he would be an excellent role model for their adopted sons. Andrew had so many more angels than she did!

CHAPTER 13

Kindred Spirits Featuring Archangel Ariel

Soon, the conversation was about their wedding. The desire to be alone with each other washed over them. They decided to go for a walk and be by themselves with their cherished memories. Their spirits had been reunited, and there was no need to talk. They mentally shared recollections of their lives together. So much love. He assured her that they would be going back to Earth together and that he would be by her side during her important mission. She was relieved to hear that, but then again, she had never doubted it.

They sat in silence as their spirits entwined with each other. The feeling was euphoric. They did not want to separate, but they knew their guests were waiting. They went back inside. The banquet table had been turned into a dessert feast. She loved chocolate, which she spied immediately. They sampled a few of their favorites. He selected key lime pie along with his favorite angel food cake. The sweet treats were the perfect ending to the banquet.

They said their goodbyes as Ariel returned to let them know what was next. "You and Andrew will spend the evening in a chalet on the side of a mountain. It has been prepared for your stay. You will not have to do anything except enjoy each other. In the morning, you will return to the banquet hall for brunch with your family and friends. Enjoy your evening together. I will see you in the morning."

All at once, they were alone in a gorgeous living room with a vaulted ceiling. A fire crackled in the fireplace, and large, puffy pillows on the floor welcomed them to settle down and enjoy the evening. Surrounded by the quiet beauty of the chalet, their minds melded into a visit down memory lane. They were back at the Ship's Wheel Inn. A drunk had fallen between them, and when they had looked up, their eyes met. From that moment on, their love on the earthly plane blossomed. Perhaps one of their guardian angels gave that guy a little nudge that night.

They had conquered life's challenges as a team. On that all-knowing heavenly plane, they understood the reasons for their silly arguments. They had always said how lucky they had been to have found each other, but then, they understood it had been destiny, their prearranged plan. They were meant to meet up at that precise time and location so they would be able to spend the rest of their earthly lives together in near perfect harmony. Looking back, it all made sense.

The sunlight faded into moonlight. They went out to look at the stars. Angie could not believe how many stars blanketed the heavens. They were millions of diamonds twinkling and nodding their welcome to the night sky. A magnificent full moon rose to join the stars. Moonbeams reflecting off the babbling brook left a glistening path. Angie was reminded of her mom, who loved the sparkling river in the moonlight that left a pathway of gems leading to her mom's front door. "It doesn't get much better than this," her mom had said. It was an evening in the company of her one true love.

They found a porch swing and nestled in together to enjoy the nighttime splendor in each other's company. The night slipped away quickly. Moonbeams were replaced by sunbeams. Flowers lifted their petals to be kissed by the sun. People were moving about. Dogs were romping to stretch their legs after a good night's rest. The unicorns were enjoying a morning drink of the crystal-clear water at the brook. Birds trilled as they welcomed a new day.

Ariel appeared and greeted them. "Good morning. I hope you enjoyed your special time together. It's time to go to brunch. Your family and friends await your arrival."

Before they could respond, they found themselves in a beautiful hall with long banquet tables. It was like entering their wedding reception. Everyone was there and seated. Welcoming smiles greeted them. The song "Happiness Runs in a Circular Motion" by Donovan ran through their heads along with the Beatles' song

"Good Morning, Good Morning, Good Morning." The brunch included Angie's favorite pancakes, waffles, French toast, and fruity syrup. She sampled them all and added a little fresh fruit—her plate was complete. They took seats at the table.

Stories of their children highlighted the conversation. Her dad told the story of how he had sent their sons rubber snakes. One of her sons had brought them to show and tell. He had made his presentation look so real that classmates ran out of the room; that had resulted in a parent-teacher conference. Angie's mom reminded everyone of how she was called Eeesh because one of her grandsons heard her name pronounced "Patreeesha."

Uncle Jim told the story of their younger son who was playing ball on the front lawn with his older brother. A competition was in full force—who could throw the ball up the highest? The younger remarked that he could because he threw his ball up to heaven and Jesus caught it and threw it back down to him. Everyone laughed.

Her mom reminded everyone of how her grandson used to say, "You're fired" long before that phrase was made popular on a TV show. At the thought of the celebrity of that show, the room fell silent. He was responsible for the escalation of the harm that had befallen the planet by undoing the great work of protecting Mother Earth enacted by those who had gone before him. He did not care about all God's children. He was a large part of the reason the earth was dying. His choices were for himself, not for the betterment of anyone else. He was the reason Angie would be leading a mass incarnation to save the loving souls before it was too late. That remembrance meant it was time for Angie to leave. It was time for her to enter the next phase.

She bid everyone farewell for the time being but assured them they would be reunited again for the planning stage of the mass incarnation. Her mom and dad shared an affectionate group hug and let Angie know they would see her before they incarnated. They had agreed to be Angie's parents again, and she was delighted. Her husband's parents shared the good news that they too would once again be Angie's in-laws. Uncle Jim bid them farewell and confirmed he would be with them always. That was all good news. Others bid them farewell and said they would see them soon. When Angie and Andrew left the banquet hall, they found Ariel waiting for them nodding that it was time for Angie to move on.

Andrew bid Angie farewell with a catch in his voice. "Goodbye for now, my love. I'll be working on our next incarnation. You'll find me in the education and planning areas when you're ready. I understand that you must complete some additional mandatory phases before we can be together again. I'll anxiously await your return when you can be by my side." He kissed her forehead.

With a tug at her heart, their spirits separated, and he was gone.

CHAPTER 14

Healing Featuring Archangel Raphael

Angie found herself in a room with Ariel. The room reminded her of an office; she saw a few desks and chairs but no windows. There were no pictures on the walls, nothing to distract them from the business at hand. It was not a cold or scary room; the creamy beige walls gave off a peaceful, warm feeling.

Ariel bid Angie farewell. "Goodbye for now, my dear one. The next archangel you will meet is Archangel Raphael. You and I will meet again, and we will work together too."

Angie's heart jumped at this news. She sincerely liked Ariel; they both loved everything about nature whether it was animals, pets, or flowers. The pink of Ariel's diamond crown twinkled as she vanished.

At that moment, Archangel Raphael was before her. He wrapped his comforting wings around her with a gentle, caring hug. His green robe was majestic. His persona emanated sympathy and helpfulness with the sturdiness of a pillar of strength. His halo was made of shimmering green emeralds. "My name is Raphael. I am known as the patron saint of healing."

"Healing? But I'm not sick, and I rested. Is something wrong?"

"I am here to make sure your mind and body are healed in preparation for your life's review. These are phases you must complete before you can plan for your next important mission."

"It will be reassuring to know I'm completely healed, but I'd like to know what you're going to do. Will it hurt? Are you going to run any tests?" Angie asked.

"Tests are performed on earthly or physical bodies. I don't perform tests. I observe by looking inside you. It's painless. You'll see and feel my green light entering your body around your mind, heart, and lower back where your chakras are. You may feel a slight buzzing. It will take only a minute or two, and then we can talk about what I find. Shall we begin?"

Instead of agreeing, Angie said, "I'd like to know why nobody answered my prayers when I was so ill with appendicitis. I prayed to God, Jesus, and Mary and said the rosary, but I kept getting sicker. Medications stopped working, and I needed another operation the day they promised I could go home. Why did they all turn their backs on me? I didn't know about archangels at that time, but why didn't they send you, the archangel of healing, to help me and ease my pain? I needed you!"

"Angie, I was with you every moment you were in the hospital and even afterward when you went home. When a larger-than-life, catastrophic emergency occurs, I can help with the smaller aspects, but I can't do anything that would affect a life's plan. Before you returned to the physical plane, you had agreed to become deathly ill to enrich your soul and the souls of others. It was your soul's choice. I cannot grant wishes that interfere with a preplanned destiny, but I can and did help ensure your comfort and minimize your pain. For instance, you did not experience pain after the first operation when you were bathed in ice for three days; that otherwise would have been torture for you. I made sure you didn't wake up until after your fever broke and the ice baths were no longer necessary. After that, you did not like cold water or cold showers because your body remembered the intense cold. I made sure you had no conscious recollection of that incident.

"The pills stopped working because the medicine they were giving you wasn't going to work in the long run. I made those drugs ineffective quicker so they would have to get the correct pills and dosage into you. When they planned to send you home, the timing was wrong. You were not ready. You became sick to your stomach, which forced the doctors to run more tests. There were problems inside you that could have killed you if you had gone home too soon. I made sure they realized you were still very ill and needed another operation.

"Remember when the window washers came in your tiny room that was full of machines and gadgets keeping you alive? The nurses chased them out of your room, so they went to the next room. I gave them the idea to wash your windows from outside and then enter your room through the window. As sick as you were, you laughed and laughed. It was my job to get you laughing. The absurdity of having workers enter from the outside worked its magic. Laughter is the best medicine.

"There were so many smaller aspects to the entire picture, but please be assured that I was right there with you. How do you think you survived after your appendix ruptured a week before you were taken to the hospital? How do you think you survived having staph, strep, peritonitis, and gangrene? Remember when the nurses would come in and ask, 'You still here?' They were all expecting you to die and go to heaven. To keep your spirit fighting, I helped you believe they were asking about when you were going home."

Angie was relieved to finally understand. She had not been abandoned. They had helped her. He had helped her. Angie was ready for Raphael to begin. She watched with anticipation as Raphael's beautiful green light entered her. She heard a faint buzzing. It didn't hurt or concern her at all. Raphael was so gentle and loving that she totally relaxed. She didn't have a care in the world. She corrected her own thought—she didn't have a care in the *spirit* world.

Raphael finished quickly as promised. "Angie, I am very happy to report that you are fine in all areas and ready to move on to your life's review. I'll see you again and often, Angie. I'll be with you to help plan your journey back to the physical realm, and I'll be with you always to keep you healthy and safe when you are on the earthly plane."

Angie was concerned about that. "What if I don't know you're there and I need you?"

Raphael was reassuring. "You'll know. I have my ways of getting your attention if I need to. I've been known to make a book fly off a bookshelf or to open a magazine article to the exact page I want you to read. I can guide you to check your electronics at a specific time by placing a thought in your mind. When you feel my hand on your shoulder, you will feel the love and care in my heart I have for you. Just ask, and I will always come to help you. I'll be monitoring you from afar, and if for any reason you need my help but don't realize it, I'll show up at your side anyway."

Raphael wrapped his powerful wings around Angie and gave her a gentle hug. He was gone. The green of his crown was the last glimpse she had of him then. Angie felt that her session with Raphael had been extremely helpful and positive. She finally understood about her serious illness and what he had done to help her. As the archangel of healing, he had reassured her that she was fine. And most important, she knew that if she needed him, all she had to do was think of him and he would come to her. It would be like having a doctor next to her always.

CHAPTER 15

Life Review—Ghost of Christmas Past Featuring Archangel Zadkiel

After her meeting with Raphael, she felt purified inside and out—a clean, satisfying feeling. She caught a glimpse of a deep, indigo-blue, glittering mist floating toward her encased in a purple glow. The colors reminded her of those that adorned the statutes of Christ during the celebration of his death and resurrection. She had come to love the archangels' beautiful wings; they came into view as the next archangel appeared before her. She knew in her heart this was not Jesus even though the colors reminded her of him. She wondered if she would ever meet him. She received an answer from an unknown source.

"You will meet Jesus when the time is right. In the meantime, you are to work with Archangel Zadkiel, whose name means righteousness of God. He will help you with a detailed review of your recent past life."

The voice had spoken in her mind even though she did not know who it was. Angie's thoughts returned to her next archangel. She would always remember Zadkiel as her Jesus angel. She cringed as she realized she was about to get a detailed life's review. Her religious upbringing labeled any wrongdoing as a sin. Confession in the Catholic church had consisted of how many times you committed each sin, not if you had committed a sin. She knew she must have committed many sins in her thoughts and maybe in her actions as well. A sense of dread came over her at the thought of reviewing her sins in fine detail.

Zadkiel wrapped his massive, strong wings around her to console her. "Angie, please remember that the Creator is love. No one is here to judge you. You will be judging your own actions. I'm here to help you understand and remind you not to be so hard on yourself. You will need to forgive yourself, and I'll help you do that. Do you remember *A Christmas Carol* by Charles Dickens?" Angie nodded. Zadkiel continued. "I helped Charles Dickens write that story to help people understand that they were responsible for their actions and that there was a better way if they allowed their free will to select a different, loving path."

Dread swept over Angie again. She started to worry that he was telling her this because she had selected the wrong path and that she had brought great harm to many along the way.

Zadkiel consoled Angie. "I assure you that was not the case during your recent earthly life. I am here with you as the Spirit of Christmas Past. Some souls must face the fact that some of their past-life choices were not made with love in their hearts. Their reviews are depressing but necessary to help them make future loving choices to clear their karma. I will enjoy reviewing your past. From the moment you were born, your soul was brimming with love. It's no surprise that you made your choices with love in your heart.

"As you witnessed from your funeral ceremony, the room was overflowing with those who loved you. You touched so many souls with your loving nature. Your caring attitude enriched the souls you encountered, and we all thank you for that. You will understand more about the impact you had on others when you view your akashic records.

"For now, I'll help you understand why you may have acted the way you did in certain situations, and I'll help you understand and see both sides of any questionable event. I assure you that there is nothing to fear. I know all the details of every minute of your life on Earth. I'd like you to start at the beginning and tell your life's story. I will remain by your side offering everlasting love and compassion regardless of any memory that may bother you."

Angie relaxed in his winged embrace. There was no use fighting it any longer. His words were helpful, but she was still concerned— she wasn't perfect. They entered a beautiful building bathed in a brilliant white light that was nonetheless peaceful, restful, calm, and pleasant. Majestic white columns seemed to stretch up past the heavens. There was a commanding presence to the building bathed in this bright but gentle light. Soft, soothing instrumental music was playing in the background. Despite its grandiose atmosphere, she felt welcomed. It was as quiet as a library. Angie wondered where they were. She thought this maybe wouldn't be so bad after all.

"Angie, we are standing in the School of Knowledge."

She was awestruck. The place reminded her of something she might find on the earthly plane, but she doubted anything could be that beautiful. She felt as if she were floating; indeed, her feet were no longer on the floor. She drifted effortlessly around the room and investigated every nook and cranny. People were milling about. Some looked very familiar, like humans dressed in earthly clothes. Others were dazzling orbs of light she knew must have been other souls.

Zadkiel said, "All the schools, and there are many, have different vibrations. The classroom known as Earth has a very dense vibration. The School of Knowledge has a higher vibration, and as a soul moves up the ladder to the different schools, the vibrations increase in intensity. At the very top, we find the highest intensity belonging to our Creator."

Angie wondered if she would ever reach that highest vibration. She had already been told she would meet Jesus when the time was right. She had been taught that God and Jesus were one and the same, so she hoped that meant she would meet the Creator too.

Raphael escorted her down a hallway with many doors. They entered one of them and were in an otherwise empty room. The pale-green walls left Angie feeling relaxed, but she wondered why there was nothing in the room.

"Angie, you have already expressed your concern about your life's review. Please remember my words. Others will not judge you. You will judge yourself with love in your heart. I will be here with you. We shall begin."

When Angie thought she would like to sit in a comfy chair, one appeared before her. She knew she didn't need a chair, but it would help her relax and would be appropriate for her life's review of the earthly plane. Zadkiel again wrapped his powerful, reassuring wings around her, and she sat comfortably in his embrace. The review began. Scenes came into view on the wall. The pictures were crystal clear with vivid colors. They were transported into some scenes, but no one realized they were there. It was just like *A Christmas Carol* as Zadkiel had said.

Angie thought back to when she first ascended to the light. She had viewed her life like a movie but in fast motion as the memories settled into her soul. This experience was different. Her mind had control of the dials or buttons. All she had to do was think *Stop*, or *Slow down*, or *Speed up* the images and presto—it happened. It was like having a TV remote in her mind. *Where should I start?* She could not remember anything before age five or so she thought. *That'll be a good starting point.*

CHAPTER 16

Life Review—Memory Lane Featuring Archangel Zadkiel

Zadkiel told Angie, "Your trip down memory lane started before you were born. You mapped out your plan for your earthbound venture prior to your arrival. Your soul mate, kindred spirit, and future husband was born six months before you. Your astrological signs and age differences were part of your agreed-upon plan."

Angie recalled that she had selected her birth date in December because she loved Christmas. Even the dreariest house came alive at that time of year with lights and festivities. Children waited for Santa, and songs of peace on earth and good will for everyone rang out. She did not feel she had earned the right to have a birthday on December 25; that date should be reserved for Jesus. Instead, she selected a date exactly two weeks before Christmas.

The plan had been put in motion when one of her soul mates and prior earthbound friend had come to Earth years before and was ready to start her family with Angie as her daughter. Angie realized why she had such a close, special relationship with her mom—they had traveled though many lifetimes together. In this lifetime, Angie was the oldest child and the only girl. Mother and daughter had the same name. When her mom had selected different names in honor of the Christmas season such as Merry, Carol, and Holly, the nuns in the hospital where Angie was born had suggested that her mom call her by her own name.

"Angie, there was some necessary angel intervention at that time," Zadkiel said. "Having the same name meant your mom would be able to stay on as your spirit guide after she had passed. You were both Sagittarians, and there was divine intervention there too. Your mom's birth date was delayed despite the predictions that she was to be born earlier in November. She arrived on Thanksgiving Day, and that year, the date was November the twenty-seventh. Exactly two weeks later, they would celebrate your birthday, and exactly two weeks after that, you would celebrate Christmas. It was imperative that the dates fell in line and that the angels did their magic to make sure it happened. You were born earlier than the doctor had predicted. That was all part of the divine plan. These commonalities—firstborn, daughter, close birthdays, and Sagittarians—set the stage for a very close relationship."

Angie had stopped the review while Zadkiel provided some details of her early life. She was feeling very fortunate and loved. She mentally instructed the review to move forward. The first part of her earthbound journey showed that she was part of a good middle-class family. She had a couple of younger brothers and friends at school, and she lived in nice, safe neighborhoods. She was thrilled that everything had turned out so well. She had a wonderful childhood surrounded by loving souls. Soon, they were up to the time when older girls were attacking her.

Angie cringed at the memory as she explained the matter. "I'd been very healthy. My cheeks were always a nice shade of red, and so were my lips. These older girls thought I wore makeup even though I told them I didn't. They weren't allowed to wear makeup. They thought I was lying. It had been humiliating at the time. They held me down and rubbed dirt on my cheeks and lips. The dirt got in my mouth and hair. My school clothes were filthy. My lips and cheeks got redder the harder they rubbed.

"They finally ran away. I tearfully made my way home not understanding why they had done that to me, and I was fearful my mom would be angry with my dirty, torn outfit. Mom was horrified, but not at me. She helped me handle the situation with the parents of the girls through the school, and they never bothered me again. I never forgot that. I didn't realize at the time that I had been bullied."

The life review moved on. Angie had been a good student, but it hadn't been easy. She had a drifting eye, and people thought she was looking elsewhere. Her mother sent notes to her teachers explaining the situation and letting them know which eye to pay attention to. Trying to get her eyes to focus together was challenging and led to severe headaches and would make her sleepy. She learned to read, nap, read, and nap again.

Even after her eye had been operated on to strength the weakened eye muscle, her reading challenge persisted. One of her eyes was good at distance while the other was good at close reading. As difficult as it may have seemed, Angie felt her limitation was minor compared to the difficulties other people had to endure.

As she reviewed her childhood, she saw a happy, content, loving, and compassionate girl. She was loved by her family and friends to whom she was sincere and devoted. She took life seriously and never for granted. She had a brush with death from that ruptured appendix when she was in high school, and from that point on, she lived every day to the fullest as if it could be her last.

When things were troubling, instead of getting anxious and concerned, she'd make a hand motion throwing her problems up to the Lord to see where they would land. Then she followed life's path forward. During the review, she could clearly see why some things happened in her life. She always knew that someday, the things she did not understand at the time would all make sense. Everything was coming into focus. She had been surrounded by love.

They moved forward to her senior year in high school when her family had moved to a different state. Angie had been devastated. She had left behind friends she had known since kindergarten. She knew she could not stay behind even though it was only a few months before her high school graduation. Initially, it was not a happy time. Looking back, it turned out to be a wonderful experience. It had been hard to transition from a regional high school to a small school, but having a younger but very tall brother on the basketball team helped. Soon, she had made new friends and had graduated and was college bound.

She had a hard time finding her path forward, but her guardian angels were there to nudge her along her way. She tried a junior college, but she took ill and had to take a leave of absence. That turned out to be permanent when she enrolled in fashion design school. She loved sewing. Her mom had given her a sewing machine when she was five. From doll clothes to her own clothes, she was a quick learner. She had a wardrobe filled with handmade items including coats and hats. Her uncle, who worked in textiles, would bring her bolts of coordinated fabrics that encouraged her creativity.

But fashion design school had not lasted long; it was boring, and she was too far advanced. So she applied to the buyers' program in a well-known department store and even modeled for the store. It was disappointing when time after time they accepted only male applicants to fill the few job openings in the buyers' program. Through all that, her mom had insisted she take typing and shorthand to fall back on. She disliked the thought of being stuck inside behind a desk, but she relented and took those classes. As much as she loved books and reading, she didn't want to struggle with her eye infliction, so on an occupational test she took, she selected all outdoor activities, and the results suggested she become a forest ranger. Contrary to the results of that test, she found herself working in offices throughout her career.

Utilizing her secretarial skills, she took a job as a receptionist for a very prominent life insurance company. Within a year, she had been promoted to lead secretary for a large group of life insurance agents. Her ability to multitask did not go unnoticed. She was a natural; she became a very fast typist. She took managerial positions with other life insurance companies. She finally felt she was on a good career path when the rug was pulled out from under her. She loved her parents and her close relationship with her mom.

When they explained to her that they were moving back to the state where she had been born, grown up, and had left five years earlier, she knew she had to go with them. A couple of her cousins welcomed her return and welcomed her into their group of friends. The transition wasn't so bad after all. She was hired as a manager for a yacht sales company. It was a positive change transitioning from telling people when they would die in the life insurance field to telling people they would enjoy their new boats in the yachting field.

CHAPTER 17

Life Review—Kindred Spirits Featuring Archangel Zadkiel

Her life review continued. It wasn't long before Angie met her future husband. Despite some challenges along the way, they had enjoyed a long marriage. One of the challenges they faced was their desire to have children, but they adopted two boys and had a wonderful, loving relationship with them.

Their later years found them tenderly taking care for their parents through illnesses and passing. Compassion had always filled their hearts. Zadkiel gave Angie gentle hugs of positive reinforcement as she recounted these major milestones on her journey through life. Had she ever lost her temper? Of course she had. She was so considerate of others that when they affronted her, she became so hurt and frustrated that she would lash out. But apologies would follow, and once she explained herself, all would be forgiven.

Zadkiel asked her about things she may have done that she worried may have offended the Creator. "What about dying my hair and piercing my ears? At times, I thought I should have been happy with the body I was given without making any changes."

Zadkiel put Angie's concerns to rest. "Those actions do not offend him. The way people dress or wear their hair are forms of decorating their bodies. Even tattoos, though frowned upon because of their permanent nature and the tendency for people to change their minds, are not considered offensive."

Angie was glad to hear that. "I was also concerned about Sundays being a day of rest, but I couldn't sit still and do nothing on Sundays."

Zadkiel put Angie's concerns to rest. "You did not offend him in that area. The purpose of that commandment was to give people a day to remember their Creator. You lived your life remembering your Creator seven days a week. The work you did on Sundays such as providing meals for your family or cleaning the house was not considered a violation of the commandment. Even when you had to work at a job on Sundays, you were doing so to earn a living for your family. You had family outings for Sundays with your children. The joy of family also fulfilled the commandment to keep holy the Lord's Day."

Angie felt very good. It was not the dreaded review she had anticipated. Instead, it helped her understand decisions she had wrestled with. Zadkiel asked Angie if she had any other concerns, but she did not. Her past-life review was done.

"Before we part," Zadkiel said, "and knowing you did an excellent job of completing your life's purpose in this and all past lifetimes, I'd like you to let me know if you have any final regrets or concerns. Perhaps something has been bothering you. A wish perhaps."

Angie was happy to talk openly about a wish that had been nagging her. "I wish I could have helped other people understand that they had their angels ready to help them at all times."

Zadkiel said, "You demonstrated your love and compassion for people time and time again. You always told people you were praying for them, and you told them to ask their guardian angels and archangels for help. You opened their eyes to what was right in front of them. You have no idea how many people reached out to their angels because of your guidance."

Angie was very pleased to hear she had made a difference. She never knew if people had taken her seriously and reached out to their angels. She was glad they did, but she still felt she could have been more forceful in this area.

Zadkiel said, "All the angels have that same frustration. All people have at least two guardian angels who help plan their lives' journeys and purpose for their incarnations. They are always standing by waiting to be asked for help. They can nudge, but they can't guide without being asked for assistance because of free will. People must choose to ask. Archangels are there for everyone at any time no matter how trivial the request may seem, but first, they must be asked, and second, the angels can give only the information and guidance the person is ready to receive.

"For example, a second grader might ask a teacher a question, and the teacher will answer in terms that child will understand. As time goes on, teachers will answer their students' questions with more details based on the grade level. The same is true right up to adulthood. You can give others information only on the level they are ready to receive it.

"Organized religions have taught so many fear-based principles that are ingrained in the minds of their followers. This was done to keep their flock following them. Certain religions will not permit their parishioners to attend other denominations' churches or marry outside their faith. However, everyone's beliefs are in their souls before they arrive on the earthly plane. If someone is baptized in one religion but later in life would prefer to practice another religion, that's fine. All prayerful celebrations of our Creator are welcomed and encouraged.

"Remember that God is love. Angels are the messengers of God's love and guidance. When people pray, they pray to the Creator, who lets his angels handle communications between heaven and earth. Ask the angels and wait for their divine guidance because it's a reply from the Creator.

"Angie, you did everything you could, and more important, you lived a loved-based life and set a wonderful example for others. You brought love, kindness, and understanding to many who needed that. Angels have the same frustrations you do. You did all you could and with unbounding love in your heart."

Angie finally understood; her nagging doubts left her. Though she was grateful the review was over, she appreciated being fortunate enough to have lived her life surrounded by love. She was free to move on to the next level where she would meet more archangels to help her on her journey toward her next incarnation. She wondered which archangel she would meet next.

CHAPTER 18

Clearing Chakras Featuring Archangels Raziel and Metatron

As Zadkiel departed, a beautiful rainbow appeared to be sliding down from the sky right before Angie's eyes. What a sight! The colors were brilliant and vibrant, not like the hazy, pale rainbows she had seen on the earthly plane. Angie loved rainbows. She used to run out after showers on a sunny day in the hopes one would appear. As the rainbow got closer and closer, Angie realized it was another archangel.

"I am Archangel Raziel. I'm so glad to hear you love my rainbows."

"I love rainbows," Angie said, "but how can you claim a rainbow as your own?"

"They are my gift to humankind. When the pressures of earthly life weigh on everyone, they need a happy break and hopefully a reflective break, so I bring forth rain on a sunny day to signal people to run outside and look to the heavens. Then I bring forth a rainbow for them to enjoy for a few moments. Hopefully, they take those few moments to thank their Creator before returning to their busy day."

"So that was you!" Angie exclaimed. "What a wonderful thing to do! I thought rainbows were a scientific event and never thought of them as a sign or better yet a pause button."

"Rainbows aren't my only mission, but they are the fun part. It's my mission to turn everyday knowledge into spiritual understanding. I help souls remember their life's missions based on the education they receive on the earthly plane. I call it practical wisdom. Sometimes, I have to develop clever and creative ways to get people's attention—thus the rainbows. I also help cut ties to past lives. I need to make sure you don't have any vows you made in a past life that are being carried with you such as a vow of poverty, self-sacrifice, or chastity. These vows from another time have no use on your future mission.

"Just sit still, my dear one, and clear your mind as you do when you meditate. If any thoughts come into your mind, take three deep breaths and exhale as you push those thoughts away. I'll be watching to see what thoughts enter your mind. I'll determine if they are connected to a past life and clear them. It's painless, but you need to be in a meditative state."

He reminded Angie of a kind, old wizard like Merlin. He had vast knowledge and a gentle mannerism with a fun, magical twist like using rainbows. Angie relaxed her body and mind and took deep breaths. The clearing began. When she heard, "We are done," she opened her eyes and saw another archangel next to Raziel with a spinning cube radiating dazzling colors.

"I am Archangel Metatron." She stared at the spinning cube high above his head. "This is the merkabah cube for healing and clearing lower energies. Its force pushes away unwanted residue."

Angie had to consciously turn her thoughts to the angel holding it. Metatron was adorned in a deep-pink color, and the cube was radiating shades of pink and green. It reminded Angie of a cross between a spinning gyroscope and a kaleidoscope with ever-changing colors. Metatron seemed like an intellectual college geometry professor with his fun toys especially compared to Raziel, the rainbow wizard.

Metatron told Angie of the need to clear her chakras. She was surprised to hear that because she thought Archangel Raphael had already done that.

"Archangel Raphael did some clearing," he said. "Since then, you have been through a life review and a past-life clearing. They leave residue that must be cleared before you can begin your research and the planning stages."

"Will you teach me how to do this myself, or will you be there with me often to do this again? My future will be full of negatives, and I'll need my heart and soul cleared many times."

"We will both be there for you," Raziel said. "However, you will be taught methods to do this by yourself that you will be able to teach others."

Angie felt relieved. Metatron gently moved the cube over her head.

"I'm starting with your crown chakra at the top of your head. The cube will continue to encircle you as it moves down in your body. The body contains many chakras or energy centers including the crown, third eye, throat, heart, solar plexus, splenic, and root or the main chakra at the base of your spine. The crown chakra is extremely important and must be kept clear so you can communicate with the angels and the divine Creator. Your crown chakra governs your ability to tap into the universe's collective wisdom and helps you make important decisions on your next mission as well as helping you while you are in your next earthly body. If it becomes blocked, you won't be able to receive clear and understandable messages.

"Everyone's body is full of chakras. There were little ones by the eyes, ears, and throat to help with seeing, hearing, and speaking. All chakras have different but very important purposes. They are all vital energy centers that must stay clear. My cube is clearing all of them for you."

The cube returned to a position above her head and glided back over Metatron's head. "The clearing is done. Another part of my mission is to provide a much deeper understanding of life's journey. During different periods of your life on the earthly plane, I'll explain what you are currently doing and why along with what you will be doing in the future and why. I'm available at any time. I'll watch over you."

Angie felt more energized. Her intuition and understanding seemed sharper and clearer.

Raziel said, "I will also be watching over you. Once you return to the earthly plane, we will visit you often to keep your knowledge pure and clean as you perform the work of the Creator. We will also meet you frequently in your dream times when Metatron will use his cube for clearing and to impart wisdom that would be helpful to you and your mission."

"I am very thankful for the clearing you both have done. I am also grateful that you will be there for me. You mentioned some methods that I could do myself. Can you teach me now?"

Metatron said, "Archangel Michael will help you with some techniques such as cutting cords and vacuuming out the negative energies. It's time for me to depart. Raziel will stay and escort you to the Tapestry Room."

Angie loved sewing. "What is the Tapestry Room? Is it a fabric store? Why would angels need fabric when they don't need clothes? If they want clothes, they just need to think them and it's done."

"Settle down, my excitable darling," Raziel said. "You will soon see."

CHAPTER 19

Tapestry Room, Library of Knowledge, and Akashic Records Featuring Archangels Raziel, Jeremiel, Haniel, and Raguel

Raziel and Angie found themselves in a beautiful room. There were no bolts of fabric as Angie had hoped. They were greeted by someone who seemed authoritative but approachable. He was dressed in a floor-length robe similar to what a monk would wear but pure white. His aura seemed to radiate through and around the robe. He held a golden pointer with an illuminated diamond tip.

Raziel introduced them. "Angie, I'm pleased to introduce you to the guardian of the Tapestry Room. This is Angie. This is a very honored place that houses the tapestry of life. The tapestry shows where everyone's lives are woven together and interconnected."

Angie was awestruck as she took in the great hall. The room was very tall, maybe a hundred feet or so. The ceiling was domed; windows encircling it let in light that illuminated the room. Immense chandeliers hung from the ceiling and emitted light from thousands of crystals intricately set where Angie would have expected to see lightbulbs. The walls and floors were highly polished marble. There were groupings of furniture for gatherings. A mild scent of flowers filled the air. Some people wore robes, some wore street clothes, and others were illuminated orbs of light. There was a hush in the room. The beams of light reflecting off everything created a dazzling but pleasant light show.

On the wall was a tapestry of millions or maybe billions of threads. Most glimmered and shined. The entire tapestry undulated as if it were alive. Some were dull strands while others were vibrant and appeared electrified.

Raziel spoke. "Each strand represents a soul and all the events that have taken place since the soul's inception."

Raziel let that sink in as Angie took in the ambiance. She noticed that the tapestry was about twenty-five feet tall and a mile or so wide. It circled the room and seemed to go on forever. Light from the upper windows and chandeliers illuminated the threads. Some of strands were very thin like pieces of string while others were as thick as cables or wrists. Sections of the strands were in shades of greens, blues, reds, yellows, oranges, and blacks.

Raziel broke Angie's reverie. "Each color represents the spiritual energy of the soul at a specific time. The black areas show when a soul ventured off life's path of love. All souls have a chance to change, to improve. When souls come to view their strands, they see where they wandered off the path. They'll see an improvement in the size and brilliancy of the colors of their threads. When they plan for their next trip back to the earthly plane, they devise ways to enrich their souls.

"Notice how each thread is interwoven. It crosses and touches other strands that touch more strands. Every soul has a direct influence on all the souls it touches. Those souls will affect other souls, a ripple effect. That is how the tapestry is woven. It is forever changing. There is a oneness among all souls. All humanity is affected by the actions of one."

"Can I see my strand?"

Raziel summoned the guardian, who pointed to Angie's thread with his diamond pointer. She was thrilled at what she saw. Her thread was a good size, nice and long, and it shimmered in the light. She saw where her thread had changed colors over time. She was grateful it had never turned black. She saw that her thread was interwoven and had touched many others over time.

"You will be able to come back later and study your stand in more detail," Raziel said. "You will want to come back with the others who will incarnate with you. You will all see how your threads have already interacted with each other. It is time to go to the Library of Knowledge, where three archangels are waiting for you."

Angie was excited. She loved being there. Everyone was so nice. Love was in the air. The places she had visited were beautiful beyond compare. She loved all the archangels she had met. "Three archangels! How exciting! They have a library? That's even more exciting! I love books but always fell asleep reading them. How many books are there? Will I have time to read them all?"

"Be patient, my dear one. We will be there shortly, and you will see."

They bid farewell to the guardian of the Tapestry Room and ascended a wide marble staircase. Raziel led the way to a hallway where precious stones including emeralds, rubies, and crystals to name a few adorned the walls; they reflected light like a dazzling kaleidoscope. They entered the library with a cathedral ceiling, multiple seating areas, and rooms along the perimeter. People were walking around with books, manuscripts, and scrolls in hand. Scholars appeared to be studying. There were precious stones on these interior walls that gave off enough light to read by. Gentle background music softened the atmosphere. There were no computers, and no one was taking notes.

Raziel said, "The souls here are not studying but researching. All information is absorbed and imprinted. It will not be forgotten and can be recalled at any time. Some are enriching their souls with new information. Others are gathering knowledge for their next incarnation. If you want to read a book, you just have to think of it and the book will instantly be imprinted in your brain. Some prefer to handle an actual book and turn the pages. That was perfectly acceptable but not necessary. You will receive the same knowledge whether you turn the pages or imprint it."

They nodded to the guardian of the Library of Knowledge, who also wore a robe and held a pointer. His pointer though beautiful was more functional and not as elegant as the pointer the guardian of the Tapestry Room had. Angie was excited to get started imprinting as many books as she could as quickly as she possible. She asked if she could begin with a huge book on a pedestal table.

"That is the akashic records book, Angie. It is ever changing and cannot be imprinted in its entirety in your brain or on your soul.

Certain bits of information will become part of your knowledge base. You will research the records of others who will incarnate with you, and they'll read your record as well. It's time for me to leave you, my dear one, in the company of three archangels who will explain more and help you on the next phase of your journey."

Archangel Raziel wrapped his wings around Angie and told her to watch for rainbows. She smiled, and he was gone.

Before her stood three tall, majestic, and radiant archangels. She recognized Archangel Jeremiel, the angel of hope. He had brought Angie through the light and for her first visit with her friends and family. He had also brought her to the resting area in the hospital wing. She was happy to see him again in his dark-purple robe with golden starlight radiating all around him.

He wrapped his powerful wings around her. "You have done very well, my dear, since last we met. I'm here to help you with the next phase of your journey, the research of your records. We'll also research the records of those who will incarnate with you. Before we begin, I will introduce you to two other archangels who will assist us in this next phase."

The first one her eyes settled on was Archangel Haniel. She was so dainty but gave off a very powerful, formidable vibration; she was a vision of elegant loveliness. A full moon seemed to encircle her head. Her aura and body were pale blue and reminded Angie of a full moon high in the sky with a halo of pale blue encircling it.

Jeremiel said, "This is Archangel Haniel, whose name means grace of God. One of her specialties is to awaken your spiritual gifts of intuition, clairvoyance—clear seeing, clairsentience—clear feeling, claircognizance—clear thinking, and clairaudience—clear hearing. You will need to develop these for your next incarnation so we can communicate with each other. As we research other souls, she will help you understand them and release them from any judgment you may have."

Haniel greeted Angie with a gentle, feminine embrace. "Anytime you need me, I'll be there for you. Every time you see a full moon, think of me sending you angel blessings. Anytime you have heartbreak or emotional pain, I'll guide you through those trials and tribulations. Trust in the feelings you receive because they will be me sending you love and guidance. I'll help you find your hidden talents and polish your skills. I will be your magical princess."

Angie wanted to hug Haniel again but could not figure out how to hug this beautiful, dainty angel with her huge wings. Haniel instantly enveloped Angie in another gentle hug. "I may seem fragile, but I'm not. Anytime you want to hug any of us, just think the thought and it will be done."

"Archangel hugs!" Angie exclaimed. "That's what I'll call them. They are so comforting and sincere. I love them! I can recall feeling hugged like this on the earthly plane, and now I know I was and by whom."

Angie turned to the third archangel. His dark-blue aura peeked through his emerald-green halo. It reminded Angie of the springtime sky peeking through the newly emerging green leaves on the highest tree branches. The blues of Haniel and blue and green of Raguel were complementary.

"I am Archangel Raguel. I am pleased to officially meet you and help you plan for your extremely important mission. My specialties are harmonizing all relationships and bringing orderliness, fairness, harmony, and justice along with forgiveness, peace, and calm. It has been determined that you will incarnate as the leader of a mass incarnation. It is time to acquaint yourself with the souls that will return with you. They have all been specially chosen by the archangels and have been approved by the Creator. When you read through their akashic records, you may come across something that will give you pause and make you question their ability to fulfill this important mission. I'm here to help you understand why certain actions were taken by certain souls and why they have been selected to be parts of your team."

"I don't want to judge anyone but instead learn who they are," Angie said. "I'm glad you're all here to help me with my research and keep my thoughts pure and full of love."

"Then let us begin," Raguel said. "We will not focus on your soul mate or parents, whom you know so well. We'll focus on others you may not know. I have a list. One by one, we will check their akashic records so you can imprint their information. When you meet these souls in the School of Wisdom, you'll know who they are in detail. Their souls have amassed superb knowledge in specific areas that will be beneficial and essential for this next incarnation. They had also gone through the resting and cleansing phases.

"Andrew has already been working with them and the angels to devise a plan of action for the mass incarnation. A draft will be presented to you and all the archangels to review and make any final adjustments to. Then the plan will be set in motion. For now, you are not to worry about the plan. Instead, you need to go through these names and read their records. Archangels Jeremiel, Haniel, and I will sense any hesitation or concerns you might have, and we'll provide you with explanations."

Angie thought this phase would take forever; there must have been a couple hundred names on the list, but it did not take long. She would look at a name and the akashic record instantly opened to the correct page. She glanced over the information and in a flash it was in her knowledge bank. She would look at the next name and the book would flip to that specific page. Again, a quick scan and the information became hers. Only a couple of times did a red flag appear to go up, but it wasn't there for long. One of the archangels explained while the other counseled her on the choice, and all was understood in no time at all.

Angie was amazed at how quickly she accomplished this task and at how much she learned about the many who would accompany her on her mission. She had felt she was up for this challenge the first time she'd heard about it, and after all the preparation, she knew she was ready for the challenge. The archangels hugged Angie one by one and bid her farewell. "Angel blessings to you, Angie. We will always be available for you. We look forward to seeing you again."

CHAPTER 20

School of Wisdom Featuring Archangels Michael, Raziel, and Uriel

Angie was not alone for long. Appearing before her was a vision of strength and power holding a mighty sword. She had no doubt—*Archangel Michael!* He appeared so quickly that he startled her; she stared at him in awe. She had called out to him every day during her previous life on Earth; she knew he had continually answered her requests. Though she had briefly communicated with him after her passing, she had only heard him, not seen him.

All the earthly artists' renditions of him did not do him justice. His mighty sword was made of pure light radiating strength and justice. His royal-blue robes and golden aura signaled authority and masculine beauty alike. He wrapped his mighty wings around her and pulled her close. She melted into his embrace.

In a tender voice, the mighty archangel said, "You are correct, Angie. I am Archangel Michael. My child, you know me so well and yet you seem surprised to see me. Don't be startled. There is no need to be. My mighty presence will help you as I've always done and will continue to do. Your mission will require powerful support. I'll always have your back. If you need to communicate with me, just think my name and your concern and answers will be forthcoming.

"You know you had three wonderful guardian angels—Arla, Reena and Ed—during your last incarnation, but there were two more you were not aware of. One was me, and the other was Archangel Gabriel. We were there with you, and though you often spoke directly to us, we didn't reveal ourselves. Our concern was that you would lean on us instead of on your very capable guardian angels. They did a marvelous job assisting you even though you didn't pay them much mind."

Angie knew he was correct. She always sent her requests and prayers to Michael, Gabriel, and Raphael as well as to Jesus, Mary, and the Creator. She felt sad that she had not interacted with her guardian angels more often.

"Angie, guardian angels never feel bad or slighted. They were there to help you regardless. They often answered your requests on our behalf. They didn't mind that you called out to us instead of them. And we archangels didn't mind if you called out to Jesus or the Creator. We all work together to help answer the requests of all souls no matter whom they call out to. You're such a kind soul. We understand why you feel you slighted your guardian angels, but don't. All is well. You remember Raziel."

Angie turned to Raziel; it was like greeting an old friend, her rainbow friend. "Yes. He helped clear my chakras with Metatron and was with me in the Tapestry Room and the Library of Knowledge."

Raziel gave Angie a welcoming archangel hug, and Angie asked, "Where are we now?"

Archangel Michael responded, "We are in the School of Wisdom."

Angie wasn't sure how they had gotten there, but they were in another magnificent area. The walls were full of precious stones of every color. Angie noticed private rooms and open areas where people were communicating in hushed tones. Once again, the ceiling was very tall with a rotunda high above seeming to reach the heavens. Windows high up let light in to illuminate the area. Sunlight bounced off the precious stones that radiated all the colors of the rainbow. And there she was with Raziel, her rainbow archangel. "This is perfect!" she said.

Archangel Michael said, "First, let us introduce you to Archangel Uriel. He will help you focus your mind and receive all the knowledge, wisdom, and understanding that will be beneficial for the mass incarnation. His name means light of God, and he connects to God's infinite wisdom."

Archangel Uriel was adorned in bright yellow including his aura. He reminded Angie of sunbeams on a clear day. Angie thus had a sunshine archangel to go with her rainbow and moon archangels.

"I am very pleased to meet you and help you," Uriel said. "You will need protection from the negatives that will come your way and, as you used to say, the boulders in the pathway of life."

Angie was startled at the remembrance of one of her coping phrases. She had avoided, or gotten around, or walked right over some of her boulders, but she had struggled with others before getting past them. Nonetheless, she eventually learned to traverse all the boulders in the pathway of life in one way or another. She knew she needed to expect them and do her best to proceed.

Uriel continued. "I'll be there to protect you along with Archangels Michael, Raziel, and all the other archangels. I am here to help you illuminate your mind with information, ideas, epiphanies, and insights. Consider me a wise old owl, and if you see an owl, know that it is me in your midst."

Angie liked the wise old owl image but was very fond of her sunshine angel. She'd know him as both. She felt his approval and agreement. *What negatives is he referring to?* she wondered. As the question crossed her mind, Michael was quick to answer.

"The negatives often come in the form of your ego, that doubting voice inside you that says you can't or shouldn't do something. Always remember that all things are possible through the Creator. Never doubt yourself. We will work hard to make sure all your thoughts are love based to make it easier for you to chase your ego away. If you are ever in doubt about anything, ask your guardian angels or any of your archangels for guidance. All people need to know it's easy to conquer their doubting egos with the help of the angels."

That made Angie feel better. She didn't like confrontations and didn't want to fight anyone. Fighting off her ego with love and the help of the angels sounded like something she could do.

Archangel Michael led Angie and Uriel to the area where they would hold their private meeting. Angie entered the room and was overcome with joy. Andrew was waiting for her at the entrance. They embraced with a longing to never be apart again. Their minds were one. They knew there would be times when they could not be together especially in their youth. They understood that they were doing this for the sake of the planet Earth. If anything happened to the planet, all the people there would perish and the entire solar system would be thrown off balance and into ruin. Many other planets were inhabited by souls and civilizations. If one were severely affected, they all would be.

Andrew let her go knowing there were others waiting for them—the core team. Angie noticed both sets of parents were there too. Her parents would bring her up, so they needed to understand her future and nudge her along the correct path. Andrew's parents were there as well; they would need to understand his future so they could nudge him along as well. When the time was right, Angie and Andrew would be reunited and would work together for the good of all humankind.

Many others were there; Angie knew them all from her review of their akashic records. Some she also knew personally from her recent earthly incarnation.

CHAPTER 21

New Earth—The Shift Featuring Archangels Michael, Raziel, and Uriel

Angie wanted to take everything in—the gorgeous angels, her soul mate, both sets of parents, her core group, and the beautiful surroundings. She felt the love in the room—love for each other and love for humankind. Her heart was filled with pure joy and confidence for the mission ahead.

Michael started the meeting. "Angie, as you have surmised, this is your core group. Raziel is here to gather all the details of your mission and help you open your mind to receive all the knowledge that will be imparted to you. There is a lot of history of the planet Earth that will be helpful to you and your group. You also must understand that earth dwellers, known as humans to you, are not the only ones who are caretakers of the earth. You have heard of UFO sightings, aliens, and extraterrestrial beings. They have been there since the earth's creation. Some of them will join us shortly. Everyone, please get comfortable and relax your mind so you can imprint the knowledge we will impart to you. Do not interrupt with questions. I'll know when a question enters your mind and the best time to answer that question. Let us begin.

"A very long time ago according to earth time, another planet Earth was created. It was a duplicate Earth without any pollution, damage, or spoilage. The new planet was Paradise, Shangri-la, the Garden of Eden, and heaven rolled into one. It was pristine. The foliage was lush. Birds, insects, reptiles, and animals lived in harmony and helped sustain the planet without human inhabitants or intervention. The original and new planets took up the same space to avoid any disruption to the intricate workings of our galaxy and all the galaxies beyond. The new Earth was not visible and could not be detected by humans. It had the same resources as the original Earth including gravity, air, water, temperature, and all the essentials needed to sustain human life on the planet."

Michael interrupted this story to acknowledge the group. "Yes, you are all correct in your thoughts and dreams of this beautiful planet. I will explain how humans came to live there. It came time to shift humans from the original planet to the new planet. Remember hearing about civilizations that were considered lost when evidence of their existence was discovered? The Mayans are a perfect example. They had made great advancements in developing their nation. Their achievements included a fully developed writing system, mathematics, a detailed calendar, architecture, art, and astronomy to name a few. These attributes provided the basis for the colonization of the new Earth. Therefore, the Mayans were selected to shift to the new planet where their skills would be utilized.

"No, not all Mayans were selected—you are correct. Some did not have love in their hearts because they had free will and made wrong choices. Only the loving souls shifted; all soul filled with negative thoughts and intentions stayed behind. They never understood what happened to everyone else, so there was no history recorded for future generations. Those who remained eventually perished or wandered off to join other communities.

"I'm sensing many questions about the Mayans, so I'll explain further. Those who shifted thought they were waking up in the same home they had always known. They did not realize they had shifted anywhere. They thought the missing ones had wandered off to live elsewhere. The shift had been organized in such a way that no one knew there had been a change. Once again, I ask that you clear your minds as I continue.

"Atlantis and Lemuria were not fictional civilizations as some believe. They were very real, and their loving inhabitants shifted to the new Earth before the waters swallowed up their homes. Those left behind who survived migrated to other civilized areas. Many good souls from seemingly lost civilizations throughout the world had already shifted to the new Earth. As with the Mayans, they woke up to a new day not realizing they were on a new planet.

"Eventually, the inhabitants of the new Earth decided to explore and came across other civilizations. They shared their knowledge as love and harmony spread. We have covered a lot of information. Let us take a break. Discuss among yourselves the glory of the new Earth. In a few moments, we will talk about what has happened to the old Earth."

Angie saw Archangels Michael, Raziel, and Uriel left the room; she guessed they had important business to attend to. She and Andrew visited with their parents. Hugs were exchanged. Everyone was in a very good mood with thoughts of Paradise on their minds.

Michael, Raziel, and Uriel soon returned. Michael stood before them like a professor teaching a class. Raziel and Uriel stood at his side. Everyone sat, and Michael continued.

"It will be helpful for all of you to understand the old Earth—how it came to be and how it turned so negative. Before they incarnated, all souls received specific instructions to cultivate the old Earth with love, but something went horribly wrong. Love was lost, and greed, selfishness, power, and disrespect for all manner of life turned some of the loving souls dark. That darkness spread over the planet like a deadly disease.

"The original plan for planet Earth had been for it to be a vacation and holiday paradise for the souls who inhabited other planets in the galaxies. It was a magnificent resort with lush, green forests and fields teeming with flowers. Majestic waterfalls and mountains reached up into the clouds. The animals were friendly and not feared. A mineral below the surface supplied the energy the travelers needed for their spacecraft. The mineral was easily mined and converted into a very powerful but light fuel. Earth was a very popular vacation spot.

"Some of the visitors liked it so much that they didn't want to leave. They decided to stay and make this utopia their home. Years passed, and visitors continued to come. Before long, there was a power struggle. Those who called planet Earth their home did not want to give up the resources that the visitors needed to power their craft. Arguments led to fights, and negativity started to spread throughout the paradise. The visitors continued to return to their vacation planet with good intentions. They shared their vast knowledge including the harnessing of solar power, growing crops, and understanding the stars.

"Pyramids were erected with the use of group levitation and tuning-fork devices allowing massive stones to be slid into place and fit like gloves. The pyramids were built in specific energy areas, and they housed the great knowledge of all civilizations. Areas were built to guide the planetary visitors to their destinations such as Stonehenge. Crop circles were frequent occurrences and were necessary to create a balance by infusing the earth with energy circulating above and below the surface. The crop-circle method of balance continues from afar to today. The beautiful designs of this energy marvel create wonder and amazement."

CHAPTER 22

Future for All Souls Featuring Archangel Michael

Angie noticed that everyone was listening intently. It was very quiet in the room except for Michael's commanding voice. She had wondered how the massive pyramids and stone structures had been made. She marveled at the precision and intricate designs of the crop circles and always wondered who could have made them. At that point, she knew.

She thought of how she had lived on planet Earth and had seen firsthand the negativity that had spread. Too many seemed to focus on enriching themselves and to plan for their future incarnations, but they weren't necessarily considering the bigger picture; many had blinders on. All they wanted to know was what was in it for them.

Michael read her thoughts as did everyone else in the group and said, "Angie, all souls must focus on their enrichment. Remember that they are learning and attending school. The students are not expected to change the world but to set a good example for others by living loving lives. It is the job of the Creator and his angels to try to fix the classroom Earth."

Angie was glad she had graduated and was no longer attending school. She was on the team and would be able to help save loving souls. Her core group signaled their agreement.

Michael said, "The desire has always been to restore planet Earth to its original concept—a paradise full of loving souls. Please understand that we all tried time and again. The weakness in the human soul has been analyzed and will not be permitted to repeat itself. In the future, free-will choices will include only loving options and will be guided by a collective consciousness. That might sound confusing, but it's not.

"Rather than having a choice between positive and negative options, the negative choices will no longer exist. Souls will still have free will, but their only choices will be loved based. Since everyone will be able to communicate telepathically, souls will collectively decide on the choice that will best suit all of them. This has been successfully tried on other planets. Hatred, lust, greed, murder, theft, and all the other negative, destructive atrocities against humankind will no longer exist."

Angie thought everyone would start clapping at this change. A world without negatives sounded unbelievable and wonderful at the same time.

Michael looked at Angie. "What I have explained might seem unbelievable but is very attainable, and so it will be. Raziel introduced all of you to the Tapestry Room, where you witnessed that all souls are part of a larger fabric, the tapestry of life. You saw times when the smallest disruption caused devastation to every soul it touched past, present, and future. Without negativity, all souls will have positive impacts on all other souls.

"Numerous times, Earth was ravished by floods and other natural and man-made disasters. Time after time, the faraway galaxies sent their residents to help restore Earth. Unfortunately, history repeated itself. Lessons were not learned. The negativity had taken hold of the souls and blanketed the planet like fog hiding its glorious vistas every day. The hope was that love would penetrate the fog and that one fine morning, all negativity would be gone forever. That has not happened, and at this point, it never will.

"The brilliant collective minds of the far galaxies have sent numerous visible signs warning of impending doom. Some paid attention while those in authority ignored the signs and let Earth continue in a death spiral. The ice caps are melting, inhabitants are wearing masks to be able to breathe, and the drinking water of an entire town is polluted and is poisoning God's children. Many saw and understood the signs. They protested in the streets. Local and foreign governments tried to handle the crisis on their own. Regrettably, those in power turned a deaf ear and a blind eye. Greed and an unquenchable thirst for power and wealth dominated and destroyed.

"There have been visitations as well. Ascended masters have been sent. Jesus came to Earth to witness the travesty for himself. He investigated one religion while others came to investigate other religions and cultures while spreading the teachings of love. These visitors came across many dark souls, but they also came across multitudes of loving souls who listened to them and followed them. The Creator does not want to destroy the planet again. It is not all bad. Many wonderful souls have returned to earth through many incarnations with boundless love in their hearts. We want to spare them the heartbreak that will enfold the old Earth.

"They need to be rewarded and saved. They deserve to live in peace and harmony. Remember that earth is a school to enrich souls. The great pyramids contain all the knowledge needed by humans to soar to great heights with accomplishments that will help all those on the planet live wonderful lives with no needs, wants, or diseases. The only requirement is that all souls must live loving lives. A mass consciousness of true love will bring ultimate power to the planet, a power that will benefit everyone equally. Until that can happen, that knowledge will be lost to them. Knowledge in the wrong hands would have a deadly impact on the planet."

When Angie wondered if there would be financial institutions and different classes of people such as the poor, middle class, rich, and wealthy, Michael responded with a resounding no. His tone softened. "Amassing wealth was one of the roots of evil. There will be no need for money, banks, or wealth thereby eliminating the class system. Every soul will be equal. There will be no diseases, no hospitals, no medicines, and no government."

Angie loved this concept—true harmony. She could tell everyone agreed with her.

Michael continued. "There is only one option left, and that is to save the good souls. Long ago, a plan was put in place to allow the old planet to die off with its negative souls and be simultaneously replaced by the new Earth full of wonderful, powerful, and loving souls. No one on either planet would feel it happening. The old Earth would be gone while on the new Earth, the good, loving souls would wake up to a paradise they so deserved and that many were already enjoying. The knowledge vaults found in the great pyramids would be opened. The future advancements would be mind boggling, achievable, and appreciated. All souls on the new Earth and from the far-off galaxies would live in harmony."

"Fantastic! That will be awesome!" Angie exclaimed, but then she felt awful about interrupting Michael; she was supposed to contain herself. But all the good news gave her the hope she had lost long ago. The others were clapping and talking among themselves.

Michael allowed the jubilation to continue for a bit. After the room quieted down, he said, "We must focus on preserving the dying planet long enough for the shift to be completed. If the planet dies before we are ready, there will be a devastating impact on all the planets in all the galaxies. Loving souls will suffer needlessly. They have done nothing to deserve the same fate as those who have ruined the planet. We must save them by shifting them to the new Earth. The shift has been working. The new Earth is full of loving souls who are living in harmony and ready to make room for more loving souls. Your mission is to help the remaining loving souls shift to the new planet."

Angie wondered how they would be able to help the loving souls. That time, Michael did not answer her. He continued with his explanation.

"The old planet is dying. The dark souls will be left behind to suffer the consequences of their actions. No matter how much money they have or how many deadly weapons they possess, they will not be able to enjoy life on the original planet. Their unbelief in climate change and environmental controls will leave them with undrinkable water and food full of cancer-causing chemicals. Rich farmland will become tainted and unable to grow crops. Ownership of the most luxurious buildings will not provide them shelter. Those who do not shift will eventually die and return to the afterlife, where they will undergo long resting and learning periods.

"And they will never be allowed to go to the new Earth. They'll be sent to a primitive planet in a far-off galaxy. This planet is similar to the old Earth as it was in the beginning. There will be no creature comforts. Instead, they will be forced to learn survival skills. They will be given another opportunity to live lives with love in their hearts. It will be a very difficult life to endure but necessary to reteach their souls. Many will never learn. Once they go through the veil of forgetfulness, many will instantly be lost again.

"But the good news is that the majority will learn and thrive with love. The Creator and his archangels will guide them. The Creator has chosen this method to once again instill love in the souls who have turned extremely dark. Do not consider this a punishment. Our Creator does not punish or seek revenge. These dark souls will receive another chance.

"I sense many questions. Will the new Earth be primitive too? Will all the inventions and advancements have to be relearned? What will clothes be like? What will the food be like? I told you I could read your thoughts, and those are good questions. The best way to explain life on the new Earth is to look at the civilization known as Atlantis before its people caused their own demise. The main part of Atlantis was so far advanced that its people were on the verge of joining the galactic community. That meant they would have been able to leave the planet, visit the far galaxies to share their knowledge, and return. They would have become part of the council representing all the inhabited planets throughout the galaxies.

"To understand this, you need to understand more about the Atlanteans and their rise with the help of the galactic community. Earth dwellers always suspected that visitors from outer space helped build the pyramids and Stonehenge, and they were correct. How else could those huge stones have been put in place? The pyramids were built in a perfect geometric triangle on all sides and are in perfect alignment with the universe. Stonehenge was built in a perfect circle aligned with the stars."

CHAPTER 23

Paradise Found Featuring Archangel Michael

Angie and the others listened intently. Michael was such a powerful and compassionate storyteller. She was elated that all souls would live happily ever after on the new Earth. Michael acknowledged her compliment and remarked that all the archangels, ascended masters, and the Creator would be very happy to see Earth restored to a loving planet. It had been a problem for eons. They could see light at the end of the tunnel, and it was a loving light. Michael explained he would answer their other questions later and went on with the story.

"Now back to the Atlanteans and other civilizations. They did not have huge cranes or machinery. The pulley and belt systems mentioned throughout history were the only methods the authors could imagine. Hieroglyphics were found throughout the entire planet that showed visitors from outer space had been on Earth and had helped. Mere humans did not have the strength. They did not have rulers cracking whips as has been portrayed in the films or books either. Instead, they had a positive collective consciousness. They could tune into and access various types of energy to create perfect stones, move them, and set them in place even if they weighed thousands of tons.

"With the power of positive thinking, they knew they could accomplish these unbelievable feats, and they did. They could not allow any negative or naysayers among them. Their collective belief was all they needed to manipulate the energy.

"They also had superior psychic abilities. As I can read your minds, they too could read each other's minds. If someone had a concern or something was out of balance, the collective energy could instantly solve the problem. They were in harmony with each other and could have achieved harmony with the entire galaxy. Unfortunately, they experimented with crystals in a dangerous method and annihilated their civilization before they achieved an intergalactic community."

Michael explained that it was time for another quick break. He still had a lot of information to give them regarding how things would work on the new Earth. Again, Michael, Raziel, and Uriel left the room. Angie and Andrew were surrounded by those wanting to discuss what they had just heard. Their pleasant exchange ended when Michael, Raziel, and Uriel came back.

Michael got right to it. "You have undoubtedly heard that humans use only a portion of their brains. The brain has a huge capacity and is composed of the mind and the psyche. The mind takes care of the essentials of life. The psyche is not developed in the vast majority of earth dwellers. The capacity for development is there, but it leaves children at a young age when they are taught reasoning and science.

"I'm sure you have seen or heard about psychics who have spoken to departed loved ones, found missing people, and predicted the future accurately. Those people have developed their psyches. Everyone on the new Earth will be able to do that as well. Eventually, they will be able communicate and travel by thought. They will not need televisions, radios, or telephones. If they want to learn something, they will think it and the answer will be provided. If they want to converse with others, they will just have to think about them regardless of how far away they are, and they will have an immediate telepathic conversation.

"They will not have governments, rulers, or leaders. Instead, they will have a keeper of all knowledge like the guardians you have met here. All thoughts and experiences will be available for review and action including information from the far galaxies based on their experiences and accomplishments. Children will still need to be taught, but the focus will be teaching them to develop and retain their psychic consciousness as they are taught the basics of life on their planet.

"Food consumption will be very balanced with fruits and vegetables, nuts and seeds. There will be no need to kill the gentle beasts that roam the new Earth. Killing for food would turn animals into a negative force against humankind, so that will not be permitted. Animals have positive attributes that will help the new Earth. The balanced human diet will prevent diseases, so there will be no need for doctors, hospitals, or medicines.

"Crystals will be become a very important part of everyday life. The galactic community will help teach their many functions. Crystals will help with their healing properties similar to laser surgery and for those who are injured by accident. They will also be used for transportation. Beams will be used as pathways for travel in conveyances such as people movers. They'll use this method to move large objects. In due time, interplanetary travel and travel to the heavens will be achieved just by thought. Think it and you will be there.

"Large gatherings will enjoy the great outdoors and each other. There will be no worries of dreaded family gatherings that include negative relatives who spoil everything. Imagine those family reunions at which everyone gets along and that is what you will experience.

"Crystals will provide lighting so there will be no need for power plants or dirty coal and oil that deplete the very core of the planet. Wind and solar energy will supplement what crystals cannot provide. The crystals that can produce lighting will come in all shapes and sizes. Some will be large enough to light up the streets and walkways at night. Many colorful crystal lighting options will have the added benefit of bringing beauty indoors.

"Water for drinking, bathing, and swimming will collect in geographically designed areas and kept clean by natural movement and aeration. The rains will come at night when the world is at rest, and every morning will dawn with a beautiful sunrise along with an abundant water supply. There will be no more earthquakes, hurricanes, tornadoes, blizzards, floods, droughts, or any of the bad weather that was a result of the negative consciousness. People expected these disasters to happen and willed them into existence. The occupants of the new Earth will positively agree that it will gently rain at night enough to fill their reservoirs.

"There will be plenty of opportunities to play and enjoy. The flowers will delight with their visions of loveliness, and their fragrances will waft on the gentle breezes to everyone's delight. I'm sure there will be plenty of other needs you will wonder about based on your recent earthly experiences, but be assured that the galactic communities will have the answers. No one will want for anything.

"We have learned the error of our ways. Free will including negative choices was the failed experiment. As I mentioned before, free will will be altered to include only positive choices. A collective positive consciousness and superior knowledge will result in positive group decisions. Individuals will no longer rise to be superior beings in their own minds. All will realize that they are part of a larger group as you saw in the tapestry of life. Everyone will work together for the good of everyone else. That was the original intention when the earth was created. Now that we have identified the greatest harm to humankind—negativity—it will cease to exist.

"The choice to wear clothing will be similar to what you find on this astral plane. You may wear clothes if you wish, and although it is not necessary, most will choose to wear outfits to fit their personalities and needs. The necessary products will be available. The extraterrestrials have developed different fabrics to protect their skin on the earthly plane, and they will share their knowledge. Human souls will collectively decide what will work best for them. The temperature will be ideal, so there will be no need for coats, boots, or any other type of warm clothing. Raincoats will not be needed unless you enjoy being out at night in the gentle rainfall. Attire will be a personal, loving choice. Over time, the need for a human form might be eliminated. Instead, all souls may choose to be orbs as they have chosen to appear on the heavenly plane."

CHAPTER 24

Extraterrestrial Friends
Featuring Archangel Michael

Angie and her group were very happy about what they were hearing. The new Earth would be a paradise beyond their wildest expectations. Michael did not sense any questions, so he continued.

"It is time to explain extraterrestrials or ETs in detail. Before we map out our plans for the shift of the loving souls who remain on the original Earth, it's important for you to understand who is included in that 'we.' Part of the we includes the Creator. We also include the ascended masters such as Jesus, Buddha, Moses, Mother Mary, and Confucius to name a few. All the archangels, angels, guardian angels, spirit guides, and others are included in that we. You and an army of loving souls are all included in the we. But that is not all. There are many inhabited planets or schools throughout the galaxies.

"You remember all the UFO sightings throughout the world in the 1970s. UFOs had always been coming and going, but during that period, they were visible, and that frightened many earth dwellers. When the sightings subsided, humans thought they were no longer being visited, but that was not true. Advanced cloaking devises shielded UFOs from view. There are huge ships and smaller ships above and below earth's surface inhabited by many species of souls who are called aliens and extraterrestrials. We will continue to use the familiar terminology ETs and UFOs.

"Some ETs are large and appear to be archangels without wings. Others closely resemble the ETs who died when their spacecraft crashed and was moved to Area 51. The mission of those souls was to depart and leave their bodies behind along with the remains of their craft for earthlings to study. Literature and films have depicted many ETs as something to fear and insinuated that they wanted to harm Earth and its inhabitants. That is absolutely not true. To avoid mass panic, the government has kept extraterrestrial discoveries a secret. ETs have a vibration and intelligence superior to that of the souls inhabiting the old Earth. More important, they are loving souls and are not capable of hurting anyone or anything.

"Before incarnating, many earthbound souls agreed to work with the ETs, but after they went through the veil of forgetfulness, they didn't recall their agreement. ETs continue to visit them frequently during their dream and sleep states when they remember their agreements. Sometimes, the humans are taken up into the UFOs, but they are returned to the same place and time with no witnesses to or remembrances of that.

"ETs are not to be feared. They are to be welcomed by you even though they look different. You and some of your core group will visit them often. You will learn from them and share your concerns with them. Archangels will help guide you and answer your requests, but at times, you will need partners in the galaxy who can use their superior skills and knowledge to assist you in the physical form.

"When you visited some of the great halls here on the astral plane, you saw some souls dressed in earthly garments while others appeared to be orbs of light. ETs have many appearances and could startle souls that are expecting to see an earthly form. Therefore, they initially appear as orbs of light. You will soon see some in their natural state. Be not afraid. They will become part of your team and will help you with their superior intellects. They will frequently visit the new Earth to offer their strength, might, and wisdom to cultivate the new planet. Angels will keep watch. When humans need help that would be better handled in a physical form, we alert the ETs.

"Many of you are wondering what will happen to the old Earth. Both planets will coexist in the same space for a long time. When all the loving souls have shifted to the new Earth, there will be a time when the negative souls must endure what they wrought on the planet. There will be earthquakes, volcanos, hurricanes, and blizzards along with the melting of the polar ice caps. There will be droughts and floods along with the invasion of insects and other vermin. Many will perish and will come here to start their extended resting period.

"Eventually, when there are no living souls left on Earth, the planet will implode. As the old Earth vanishes from sight, the new Earth will immediately shift into its place. There won't be any disturbance to the galaxy or the finely tuned orbits of all the other planets. The souls on the new Earth may feel a slight disturbance in the force, but it will be over very quickly, and life on the new planet will go on."

Angie asked, "Is there any chance that any of the negative souls can still be saved?"

"It is never too late for lost souls to fill their hearts with love and become part of the shift to the new planet, but you will be amazed at how many dark souls will remain clouded with their lust for wealth and power and their diminished capacity to love. Do not waste your time with them. Spread the love and kindness to as many as you can by being the gentle, loving souls you are. Call on the archangels to help those souls with sparks of love in their hearts. The old Earth still has negative free will at work, so we can only suggest and encourage. If the souls will not listen, they'll perish and come here to rest and learn."

Michael shifted the topic to ETs. "All ETs have different specialties. They will have assignments that will be invaluable to the mission. Some will be part of your core group. They come from different planets, and their appearances vary depending on that. They will be visible to all on the new Earth. However, they will not be seen by those on the old Earth because of the unfair negative reputation that precedes them.

"If you need an audience with any of them, call out to them in your thoughts and they'll find the best way to meet with you. They may be able to meet with you in person and in private, or they might prefer to transport you to one of their craft. They communicate through thought as we do. Many have large eyes that give them the ability to see a wide range as well as into and through matter. Eyelids would hamper those abilities, so their eyes have built-in protection. From a single vantage point, they can see up and down the California coast from San Diego to San Francisco and all the way out to Hawaii.

"Some have a protective skin while others wear protective suits. They do not need computers to store their information. All knowledge is imprinted in their brains to be recalled as needed. The ETs have homes and families in faraway galaxies. They can travel great distances just by thought. Some do not reproduce in the same way earthlings do. Some women have eggs outside their bodies that the men fertilize. Often, the new souls are put into incubators until they reach birth age. This gives the newborns a sterile environment with all the nutrients they need. Thus, they are disease free and fully formed in body and brain.

"They have very close relationships with their soul mates through a melding of their spirits. It is more powerful than any love or coupling you have ever known on the earthly plane. Their incarnations are carefully planned. They do not go through the veil of forgetfulness. By the way, on the new Earth, the veil of forgetfulness will be dispensed with. All people there will always be totally aware of their loving mission.

"We have covered a lot of information. Let's take a dinner break before I introduce you to the ETs. They will gladly answer any questions. Remember that they can read your thoughts, so do not be surprised with their instant responses. Raziel and Uriel will accompany you to the banquet hall where you socialized after you arrived and after your resting periods. They will sound the bell when you are to return. Enjoy."

CHAPTER 25

Pleased to Meet You Featuring Archangels Michael, Raziel, and Uriel

In an instant, the entire core group was seated in the banquet hall with plenty of food and drink. Angie noticed that different dishes were appearing in front of people. She wished for a cheese pizza, and it appeared before her.

Andrew asked, "How did you get pizza?"

"I just wished I had pizza and there is was!" Angie said.

Andrew caught on quickly; his favorite dishes appeared before him one after another.

"I'm so excited to meet the ETs," Angie said. "We always wished we could meet them. Remember the UFO that darted in front of us one night?"

Andrew just nodded; he was too busy eating to talk.

As soon as the guests finished eating and sat back in their chairs, a bell sounded. Raziel and Uriel entered the banquet hall and announced it was time return to the School of Wisdom, where some special guests were waiting for them. Angie was eager to return. Instantaneously, they were seated and ready to begin.

Instead of standing next to Michael as they had done before, Raziel and Uriel stepped back to make room for the ETs. A magnificent ET appeared next to Michael. He resembled an archangel but without wings, halo, or aura. He was tall and stately, and he exuded power. His protective covering was pure white. His large oval eyes were kind and very expressive. Angie was not afraid. She sensed a lovingness that Archangel Michael had mentioned.

"Greetings! My name is Legna. I am very pleased to meet you and have this opportunity to give you some information. We may look different from how we were portrayed on Earth. The modifications to our bodies give us increased powers. The fingers on our hands, the texture of our skin, and our lack of ears are not to be feared but understood. We do not need ears to hear because we hear with our minds. We can appear to you on earth or bring you to our ships. No one will see us because we can bend time. You are returned to the same space and time you left. We have always hoped that we could become friends and not frighten humanity. We are totally dedicated to our Creator. You will find that we are honest and straightforward. Our mission as directed by the Creator is to help the souls on earth make the shift to the new planet and assist the inhabitants of the new Earth with all their needs.

"There are as many different types of ETs, as you call us, as there are different types of humans on Earth. We come in all shapes, sizes, and skin tones. Regardless of our appearance, we all have unconditional love in our hearts and the desire to help our Creator help you. We are skilled in different tasks. All tasks are very necessary and required by the Creator.

"At some point, after your souls have returned to earth, we will insert a tracker in you. It will be painless. It is not used to track your every move. It is triggered by a fight-or-flight response and a change in your adrenal glands. When you are in danger, we will know, and the tracker will help us find you. That will give you added security knowing we can be by your side instantly and offer help on earth. Trackers will not be necessary on the new Earth, and they will not show up on X-rays or on any of your scanning machines."

Angie saw Archangels Michael, Raziel, and Uriel nod in agreement. Angie wondered why they needed trackers when the angels were with them. She also worried that this gorgeous being might die before she got to earth and had a chance to grow up. Her concerns were heard by all.

Legna addressed these concerns. "The trackers give you additional protection. They alert us in the event you need a physical presence at your side. We will be communicating with your angels instantly if a tracker goes off. Immediate assistance will be provided. Do not worry. We are not going anywhere. ETs do not die as you know death to be. There are times when ETs will be promoted to a higher vibrational plane and will want to exchange their bodies for new ones. It's like changing clothes. We will all be there for you as you see us now. Our mission is to help you, Angie, and all the loving souls who are working directly or indirectly with you.

"I overheard Archangel Michael mention the orbs you have seen. Those are ETs who have come here to gather more knowledge just as you do during your dream times. Now that you have met and communicated with me, you will recognize me in the future through our thoughts. The more of us you meet, the more of us you will recognize. You won't have to remember our names or physical appearance. Telepathically, you will know who we are.

"When you visit our ships, some of the archangels may meet you there. There are many rooms on the ships with different purposes. One of them is called the Sacred Room, where the angels bring messages from the Creator. Most of the time, messages will be delivered as instructions to us that we will pass on to you and your group. However, at times, the angels will want to communicate with you in person.

"There are also schools on the ships in which you can learn about a variety of topics such as sound, light, and energy—anything you are interested in. The lessons are taught and overseen by instructors. This interaction gives you hands-on experience in the physical form. On the heavenly plane, you gather information and guides help answer your questions. However, there is a lot to be said for physically doing things that you'll be able to do on our ships.

"Most times, your soul mate will travel with you to one of our ships or to the heavenly plane. Your core group will have many tasks, but the two of you will often travel as one. You will give each other strength. At times, you will meet in the Molecular Room where you dematerialize and your spirits entwine—a euphoric feeling. When you materialize again, your relationship will be stronger than you ever thought possible. The two of you will be one. The Molecular Room will give you that total experience."

Angie was eager to experience the intertwining of their spirits in the Molecular Room. She wondered how it could surpass what she and Andrew had experienced on the astral plane. Love was everywhere. It was such a splendid feeling. Humanity needed to experience unconditional love. Love was the answer, and it was easy, but she wondered how she would spread the message of love to millions of people.

Archangel Michael fielded her concern. "Do not worry. The message of love will spread from one to another and on to their family members and friends. Love will be contagious. The more people who experience love of everyone, the more it will grow. All good souls will hear your message of love. If you miss a good soul, we will help. Don't worry if dark souls do not heed your message. Some never will, and they will not shift to the new planet. They will be left to suffer the end of the planet as they know it. It is a lesson they must experience to realize what they have done."

Legna continued. "You'll meet many who look like me. You'll think of us, and we'll come to you. We are not like the archangels, who are multidimensional. We can be in only one place at a time just like you. Therefore, if you need help and I cannot rush to your side, I may send another ET. Don't be concerned. You will know that the ET who has come to you has been sent by me, the voice for many. I'd like you to meet another group of ETs so you will recognize them."

Appearing at his sides were two smaller ETs who resembled the pictures from Area 51. Angie wondered how she would tell them apart. Once again, she instantly received her answer from Legna. "Their outward appearance is the same, but once you communicate with them, you'll know who's who."

Angie turned from one to the other, and they welcomed her. She discovered she could tell them apart telepathically. They had love in their hearts and eyes; she liked them a lot. Archangels Michael, Raziel, and Uriel said they had to leave to plan for the mass incarnation and shift.

"Wait! Please wait!" Angie blurted out. "How do I cut cords and vacuum out negative debris? Can you let us all know how to do this? Archangel Metatron said you would explain how that was done so we can clear any negative residue on our own."

Archangel Michael replied, "Good idea, Angie. Let's do this as a group. When you meet up with other souls on the earthly plane, they sometimes attach themselves to you. They don't mean to. You help them or associate with them, and a cord is formed. Over time, these cords can wear you down, and they are not necessary. Everyone, take three deep breaths, and on the exhale, blow out any negative thoughts. Think of loving thoughts, and put a smile on your face.

"Now, hold your hands above your head and state that you would like to cut all your cords. Move your hands down to your shoulders, extend your hands out to your sides, and swing your hands to the front and back of your body as you move down the length of your torsos. That is all there is to it. All cords are cut except for the loving cords such as the ones that attach you to your kindred spirits. Those can never be cut providing they stay loving. If love turns sour, they will be cut through this method."

"That was awesome," Angie said. "Thank you. What is the method for vacuuming out debris? Should we do that too?"

Michael continued. "Definitely. You should do both, and Metatron and others will help you with their clearing techniques. The cord cutting removes the connection between two souls. The vacuuming takes care of the unneeded residue that collects in your chakras. If you witness an accident or see a scary image on TV, those thoughts linger. You want your chakras to be kept clear so you can communicate with your highest source, the Creator, and with us, the archangels, angels, and with other like-minded souls. Clean chakras help you with your intuition, clairvoyance, clairaudience, clairsentience, and claircognizance.

"Let us do this together. Put one hand above your head and imagine a vacuum in that hand. Press that vacuum to the top of your head and switch it on in your mind. Feel the gentle suction pulling out the residue from the bottom of your feet and through all your organs and chakras and then out through the top of your head. Turn the vacuum off and imagine a thick, white paste in your hand. Direct your hand to push the paste down into your body to fill all the voids created by the vacuum. Lift your hands and imagine the opening sealing up, and you are done.

"You can do these cleansings as often as you like. Don't be compulsive and do them too frequently—weekly is fine. However, do it immediately after you have had an argument or if you have a negative image in your mind. You can do this when you are lying down. Just imagine doing the motions. That works just as well."

Angie's group had all participated; she saw by their expressions that they were happy with the results. "That was so easy, and we all thank you," she said. "Shouldn't all souls do the cord cutting and vacuuming?"

"Absolutely," Michael said as he turned to leave. Angie followed Michael, Raziel, and Uriel into the hallway. They gave her archangel hugs and told her they would see her again. With a nod, they were gone. Angie returned to the room and said her goodbyes to both sets of parents, who then left to finish their plans to incarnate as Angie's and Andrew's parents.

Andrew gave Angie a big hug and said, "I know you must finish meeting with the archangels, but don't worry. We will be together again soon. I love you. If you miss me, remember that I'm always in your heart."

With a kiss, he was also gone. Everyone left to attend to their tasks, and she was alone.

CHAPTER 26

Field Trip to Earth Featuring Archangels Sandalphon and Ariel

Angie was alone with a myriad of thoughts. She already missed Andrew. Out of the corner of her eye, she saw an archangel gliding toward her. His aura was an inviting shade of turquoise like a shimmering tropical ocean. Musical notes bounced around him like colorful fish frolicking on the gentle waves. There were the faint sounds of music in the air. He was so tall that he seemed to reach up to the rotunda.

"I am Archangel Sandalphon. I am known as the archangel of music. I understand you like archangel hugs."

He wrapped his massive wings around Angie in a calming embrace. That was what she needed after her informative but very emotional meeting. She needed to get Andrew off her mind and get down to business. She said, "I thought all the archangels' names ended in the letter *l* like Michael, Raphael, Gabriel, Azrael, Ariel, and so on. Why not your name?"

"My name means cobrother. I lived on Earth with Archangel Metatron. After our very important missions there, we were taken to heaven and given our titles and duties as archangels. I am a brother to Metatron and to all of humanity and all souls. Angie, my brother, I'm pleased to meet you."

Angie was not used to being called a brother, but it seemed to make sense. "Hello." She smiled and asked, "Why do you have musical notes all around you?"

"They help others recognize me. All love-based songs are gifts from the Creator. I'm very fond of celestial music, and I like to work with musicians who sing praises to God. More important, I like all music with messages of love. It doesn't matter if it's rock 'n' roll, rap, or country and western. Love songs are universal. Archangel Gabriel is the archangel of communication. We work closely together. He helps musicians get the message of love into their lyrics, and I help with the musical composition."

Angie found that interesting but wondered what it had to do with her mission. As before, her thoughts were answered.

"Good question, Angie. You and I will visit Earth now. Archangel Ariel will join us because we will be visiting with the elementals or lower vibrations including plants and animals and many earth dwellers considered mythical such as fairies and leprechauns. That is Ariel's domain, so she will provide more details. We'll enjoy befitting music along the way.

"When we meet with the leprechauns, an Irish jig will be appropriate. Some flute music will serenade the fairies. They love to dance. We will visit some humans, and yes, we will stop in and see how your sons are doing. They will not be able to see or speak to you, but you can let them know you are there by putting the thought in their minds."

Angie was thrilled that she would see her sons. She was also looking forward to seeing Ariel. The last time she had seen her was during her family and friends reunion. Angie wanted to know why the mythical souls were hidden on Earth. *Why don't they show themselves? Are they afraid of being criticized or considered second-class citizens? Why doesn't 'Love thy neighbor' include every soul? Why do so many people claim to be part of a religion and yet treat each other so unfairly? Perhaps Sandalphon and Ariel can help me understand why,* she thought.

"I can explain," Sandalphon said. "I understand because I lived on Earth as a human before coming to heaven. Religious persecution has brainwashed people. Souls have given their power to the church. They go to church, repeat memorized prayers, and trick themselves into believing they are talking to God or their makers. It's a ritual, something they believe they must do, so they get dressed, go to church, sit in their favorite spots, look at who's there and what they are wearing, kneel, stand and sit on cue, shake the pastor's hand, and consider themselves done until next week.

"There's one thing missing—love. Did you ever walk into church and say, 'I love you, God. I love you, apostles. I love you, angels. I love you, fellow parishioners. I love everyone everywhere'? We can go through the motions of attending Mass. Many find comfort in that, and that's fine. But they must remember to keep love in their hearts, and church is the perfect environment to focus on love.

"However, when something goes wrong in their lives, they plead to their makers and ask others to pray for them. Why do they wait for heartaches? Some thank God when things go well as if God bestowed a gift on them. 'Thank you, God, for my good grade, or this beautiful day, or for winning a race or an easy ride to work.' They are superficially connecting to the source. They don't raise their consciousness and reach to heaven from their hearts. Don't misunderstand—it is always suggested that you thank the Creator for your blessings, but you must sincerely mean it. People profess to love God, but they don't feel the overwhelming love parents have for their children or the love of a young couple for each other. That's the love everyone needs to feel about the Creator and each other."

Angie understood. She felt guilty of that herself. She has felt more love since she had arrived there than she had ever felt on Earth except maybe her love for Andrew.

Sandalphon continued. "It's important for all to reclaim their connection to the source, the divine power—God. They can do this on their own. They must live by love and follow the Ten Commandments because they guide us to love. Follow the guidance in the Bible and other religious books as they pertain to love—love thy neighbor, do unto others, and so on.

"Don't chase money. Don't be greedy. Follow the love that will eventually bring you home to the lap of God. Your thread in the tapestry of life will radiate love and its positive effects on all the threads it touches. Go to church if you like organized religion but only if you remember to love. The goal is to reach out to the Creator, the archangels, and all the angels and to live in love.

"The angels are there for everyone, but egos get in the way, and free will makes it easy to follow the ego. Angie, you have unbounding love and compassion for everyone. You will return to Earth as an earth angel as you wait for the shift to commence. You will help others see that love is the answer."

Archangel Ariel appeared at Sandalphon's side. She looked like a princess all pretty in pink from her halo and aura to the hem of her gown. Ariel enfolded Angie in her wings in a loving embrace as they communicated their happiness at seeing each other again.

Sandalphon said, "Angie, your heart is full of unconditional love for everyone. My lecture was to help you see what we see from this side. People need to feel love and compassion. You will help them understand what true love is. Once they all have love in their hearts, those who have remained hidden will come out of hiding. Leprechauns and fairies will dance with humans, and the tree people will show their faces. It's time for our trip to Earth. First, we will visit your sons."

Angie was ecstatic. She found herself in one of her son's living rooms. It was lunchtime; 12:11 to be exact. That had been Angie's birthday. Her son noticed the clock, smiled, and said, "Hi, Mom!" Angie was thrilled and melted at his smile. He looked great; he was doing fine. In an instant, they were in her other son's kitchen. It was still 12:11. He noticed the time, smiled, and said, "Hi, Mom." She was elated. She missed her sons so much, but she knew she would see them again. Regardless, there was a hole in her heart. They had incarnated with her many times before.

Angie was immediately back with Sandalphon and Ariel. Ariel said, "Angie, you will assist me with the elementals, the souls who usually cannot be seen by human eyes including leprechauns, fairies, pixies, gnomes, elves, tree people, rock people, and others."

Angie wondered how she would be able to see them. Ariel said, "At some point, you'll be granted the gift of elemental vision, Angie. Until then, you'll be given ways to see them when no one else can. On this journey, you will be able to see them. I will introduce them to you so they'll be able to recognize you, trust you, and understand they are to follow your instructions as well as the instructions from the archangels, including me.

"Elementals are pure of heart, and they will all shift to the new Earth. There, they will come out of hiding and be seen by all. They'll continue to take care of all nature. When it comes time for the elementals to shift, I will let you know if I need your help."

Off they went to Ireland, where Sandalphon's musical notes turned green and an Irish jig filled the air. The music brought forth every kind of St. Paddy's Day leprechaun she could imagine. They were a jolly folk and welcomed Angie unconditionally. They danced around her as they sang out, "Top o' the morning to you, Angie!"

"And to you!" Angie replied as she joined in their merriment.

After Ariel spoke to them in private, in a chorus, the leprechauns bid them farewell with an Irish blessing: "May the road rise up to meet you. May the wind be always at your back. May the sun shine warm upon your face; the rains fall soft upon your fields, and until we meet again, may God hold you in the palm of His hand."

"Thank you," Angie said. "That blessing has never meant so much to me as it does hearing it directly from you. I wish you the same. Before we know it, we will be together again and all the loving souls will be able to see and dance with you. Until then, angel blessings to you all!"

Ariel and Sandalphon whisked Angie off to meet the tree people. The trees stood stoically as their branches caught the wind. At first, Angie saw only a forest, but when Sandalphon started to play a woodland tune, their bark faces appeared in their trunks. She thought of the trees that had thrown apples at Dorothy and those that had helped the hobbits. She loved trees and never had any idea that there were beings hiding behind their rough exterior. She loved trees more than ever.

Ariel spoke to them in private. When she finished, the trees bowed their limbs in a grand gesture toward Angie. In gruff voices, they said in unison, "We will provide a habitat for the woodland creatures, help clean the air, and provide wood for building, but most of all, we will always have your back."

Angie bowed to them as she wished them well. She received the same welcoming reception from every group they visited. She loved them all for their uniqueness. It was nightfall, the perfect time to end their outing with the fairies, who slept all day and partied all night. Sandalphon's musical notes had turned into bright colors, and the sound of flutes filled the air. There before them were fairies in a fairy circle dancing merrily. They stopped, welcomed their guests, and went right back to their frolicking. They were dainty, graceful, colorful, and loving. They encircled Angie in dance and wanted Angie to join in. She was afraid she might step on them, so they fluttered up to Angie's shoulders and danced rings around her. Angie's feet moved in time to the music, and laughter filled the air. It was a joyous moment, but soon, it was time to go.

Ariel had instructed all the groups that they would receive instructions from Ariel or Angie. When it was time for them to shift, they must cooperate and go instantly.

Angie had had no idea that all these elementals existed; she had thought they were all fantasy, so she was happy to see them. It was great news that they would soon all live in harmony with the humans and ETs.

With a hug, Ariel told Angie it was time for her to go. They would meet again, and she would always be available to help Angie.

CHAPTER 27

Meeting the Creator Featuring All Archangels

The music turned celestial as Sandalphon told Angie, "Your soul is progressing beautifully. Before you finalize your plans, you will have a special audience. You'll meet the magnificent energy that is behind everything on the earthly, physical planes as well as on the mystical, astral planes—the Creator, the ultimate wizard. You were the one and only recommendation of his archangels to save the loving souls. He has reviewed your akashic records and your cord in the tapestry of life. He agreed a hundred percent with our choice. You have been granted this unique opportunity because of the advanced state of your soul."

Sandalphon gave her an archangel hug and said, "Every time you hear music, I'll be near. Wait here for your escorts to take you to your Creator." With a smile and a nod, he left. Angie saw the musical notes and heard joyful music as he vanished.

To her total shock and amazement but also delight, her escorts were Jesus and Mother Mary. Jesus stood before her, and she went down on her knees. He extended his hand, pulled her up, and gave her a welcoming and sincere hug. He was pure love, and she never knew she could love anyone as much as she loved him right then. Her heart was bursting with sheer elation. Tears of joy welled up.

She almost lost her composure when Jesus said, "Angie, I'm proud of you. You've lived countless lives on Earth with love in your heart. You've never lost your way. You've been a wonderful role model for those who were fortunate to have crossed paths with you.

We all have great confidence in you and your group as we move forward to complete this important mission."

Angie was tongue tied, but she knew Jesus could read her mind because he gave her another hug and told her she did not have to say anything because he knew, he understood. Angie relaxed. She realized she would meet the Creator but was speaking to Jesus. They were one and the same. *How can that be?*

They were still in the magnificent School of Wisdom. Jesus indicated for her to take a seat and took one next to her. "Angie, you are so wise, and yes, you are correct. You now understand that the vibration of the Creator is so high that we have created archangels to be our messengers so we can communicate with souls of a lower vibration. Occasionally, we communicate directly with them. I was created as a recognizable being to meet and greet souls as you and I are doing now. Your vibration cannot be raised to the highest vibration allowing you to communicate with the Creator directly or you would not be able to return to Earth and communicate with human souls. I will remain in my human form so you can communicate with me as Jesus and as the Creator. You will see what I mean shortly and understand."

Angie remembered that Mary was standing there, and she felt awful she had not acknowledged her presence. Angie jumped up and extended her hand to Mary as she apologized. Mary embraced her in a motherly, comforting hug and said, "You have always kept me close in your heart. When you adopted your sons, you asked for my help to keep them safe until they could travel to be in your arms. I was happy to do that for you, and I remember how you kept their pictures tucked in a Mary figurine. You carried that figurine with you from your desk to your nightstand and everywhere you went. Since you were a child, you always thanked me and included me in your prayers."

Angie agreed that Mary had always been very special to her; she wished all people would realize Mary was there for them regardless of their religious affiliation; all they had to do was ask. Angie couldn't believe she was in the presence of Jesus and Mary and was on her way to meet the Creator. She didn't believe she was worthy. She wasn't Mother Teresa; she was just an ordinary soul who tried to live a good life.

Their thoughts intermingled on the speechless plane, and Jesus reassured her. "Angie, you carefully planned your soul's path and have fulfilled your journeys with love in your heart. You earned this right. We need someone who had successfully completed all incarnations. We need someone who does not appear extraordinary and therefore can relate to the masses. Most important, we need someone who has nothing but love in her heart. You have all those attributes.

"Special blessings will be bestowed on you and Andrew—clairvoyance, clairsentience, claircognizance, and clairaudience. You'll see and hear the angels and us while you're on the earthly plane. You'll come back to visit us during your dream times. We will always be by your side."

Angie knew she could complete her mission with all the help she had been promised. Jesus announced it was time to meet the Creator. "The archangels will be there too. They are ready for us. It will be a glorious reunion."

Jesus and Mary took her hands as they transcended to the highest plane. Angie felt an intense pull on her energy. It felt as if a giant magnet was pulling her upward to the farthest reaches of heaven. They arrived. Brilliant colors were swirling around at random. The purest form of energy was everywhere. *If only all souls could experience this*, Angie thought. The Aurora Borealis gave earth dwellers a mere glimpse of the beauty she was witnessing. She felt an overwhelming love; she loved everyone and everything. There were no negative vibrations, doubts, or ego anywhere. The visuals were awesome. She never wanted to leave. She was receiving thoughts of gratitude and praise for her achievements during her earthly lives and her intense study between lives. This is what she had lived and died for, and there she was experiencing the Creator, who was pure energy, light, and love. There was no judgment, punishment, or fear and nothing that resembled organized religion.

When they taught that God was love, Angie had seen hearts and thought of Valentine's Day. That was nothing compared to what she was experiencing. Each vibrant color represented an archangel swirling and intertwining with the others. They were always with the Creator. Archangels were multidimensional; if they wanted or needed to, they could be everywhere and with everyone at the same time. It made sense that they were always with the Creator.

Billions of stars twinkled at different intensities. As Angie marveled at the sight, Jesus explained that the stars were all the souls. Angie wondered if she was one of the stars, and she was assured she was. She was communicating with the source through Jesus; that had been beyond her wildest dreams. His essence filled her soul. She was experiencing understanding, compassion, and every other loving emotion. She returned those feelings to the source and sensed the Creator's approval and appreciation. It was breathtaking. She was one with the source. She had been taught that all souls were one with the Creator, but words could not express how magnificent it felt to intermingle her soul with the Creator's. Angie was elated.

Jesus said, "All souls are light, and regardless of where they are—heaven or earth—they shine before the Creator. The brighter the star, the higher the vibration. The dimmer ones are learning or working out their karma."

The twinkling stars were breathtaking; she was happy that so many were very bright. That gave her hope that there was more love in the world than negativity. She felt relieved. Her mission would be to bring those earthbound stars to the new Earth, and her confidence increased with the reassurances of those around her.

The archangels appeared to be playing joyfully with each other. Their colorful energies bobbed and weaved like kites swirling in the wind. Michael's royal blue and purple swirled around Gabriel's copper color. Raphael's emerald green swirled around them both. Sandalphon's turquoise swirled right through Uriel's yellow. Ariel's pale pink swirled through them all. Raziel's rainbow colors intermingled with Haniel's moonlight and Jeremiel's shooting stars. Azrael's creamy white, Jophiel's pinks, and Raguel's green swirled with Zadkiel's purple. Metatron's cube rotated around the room. She knew and recognized them all except the one with a leafy-green aura. The light show these wonderful archangels were putting on was beyond her wildest imagination. Angie wanted to swirl right through them, but she was there as an observer. She hoped someday to witness the archangel light show and dance with them, but she was content to soak up the amazing colorful sights and pure, loving vibrations. She could not speak. There was no conversation, but there was communication. They were all welcoming her and letting her know her final earthly journey would bring her home at an advanced level where she would be content for all time.

Amid the blankets of stars and swirling colorful energies of the archangels was the energy of the Creator, the most brilliant light. It was as bright as the sun but as gentle as a ray of sunlight. The energy field was intense but not hurtful. The white light had sunbeams radiating in all directions that filled the universe with gentle, powerful rays of pure light and love. This was the source, the Creator. This energy started creation and the birth of every soul; all the light particles were the souls. It was an unbelievable sight. She wanted every soul to know they too could have this experience; all they needed to do was love thy neighbor, thy self, and every living and nonliving thing. Love the environment. Love the air. Love the water. Love their food. Love their blessings and opportunities.

If everyone's heart were filled with love, there would be no anger, hurt, jealousy, hatred, or egos. All the negative emotions would be overpowered by love. It seemed so easy, but the human ego and free will had taken over love. She was glad that the new Earth would be filled with loving kindness.

She was anxious to plan her mission and go back to the old Earth to instill love everywhere she possibly could and bring the loving souls to the new Earth. A sense of duty brought her to her senses. Mentally, she thanked the Creator, the archangels, Jesus, and Mary for that wonderful opportunity to experience pure love and for their pledge to help her and all the loving souls. She would never forget that experience. They thanked her, and she found herself being pulled down, down, down.

CHAPTER 28

Mission Prep—Strategy for the Return to Earth Featuring Archangels Metatron, Raziel, Raphael, Ariel, and Jophiel

Angie was bursting with excitement and full of love. Sandalphon met Angie and gave her a huge archangel hug to settle her down. His multicolored musical notes were playing a pleasant, hypnotic melody.

She cried out, "I saw you! You were there! Wasn't it fabulous? That was the best experience I've ever had. I didn't want to leave! All those stars! The beautiful colors of the archangels swirling around not to mention the Creator. Wow! Unbelievable!"

Sandalphon replied in a calming tone, "Settle down, my dear one. Yes, I was there and experienced it. I felt the same way you do the first time I was granted an audience with the Creator. I am privileged to always be part of these meetings. I especially love to see the joy it brings others. Now, we must get back to business. We're going to the Processing Center, where details of incarnations are coordinated. It is a gathering place for souls where they make sure they understand and agree with everyone else's plans before they leave this astral plane. Remember, every incarnation must be arranged like an orchestra. Every detail must take place on cue."

Angie thought it was befitting for Sandalphon to reference an incarnation as an orchestra; the analogy was perfect. The Processing Center did not have the majesty of the places they had visited before. It reminded Angie of a library without books. There were groupings of comfortable chairs around wooden tables. People were engaged in hushed conversations. She saw a spirit guide with a plain old pointer directing people to tables and wondered which he would direct them to.

Sandalphon gave Angie an archangel hug as he bid her goodbye. "Angie, I wish you angel blessings. When you hear a song about love or praise to our Creator, I'll be close. Watch for musical notes!"

She again saw his musical notes in beautiful changing colors playing what sounded like a piano as he faded. She saw her dear friends Metatron with his cube high above his head and Raziel radiant in his rainbow colors. She wondered what they had in store for her next.

Metatron explained matters. "My job is to help prioritize your tasks and work out all the details. I have some ideas that might be helpful."

Raziel said, "I'll oversee the archangels and angels ensuring harmony and order among them to fulfill the plan. They will be overseeing your work on the earthly plane. The mission must be perfectly coordinated."

Angie thought, *Like an orchestra.* "Exactly" they responded in unison.

Instead of pointing as Angie had anticipated, the spirit guide ushered them to a secluded area that reminded Angie of a comfy den. Tufted chairs sat around a kidney-shaped, sturdy, wooden table. That configuration put everyone close to each other. Raziel and Metatron stepped to the side, and both sets of parents came into view. Angie smiled her greetings to them and turned to see her beloved Andrew. She ran into his arms. It seemed they had been apart forever though Angie knew that wasn't so. Their embrace was interrupted by a *tap, tap, tap* on the podium.

Raziel spoke. "You may be surprised that the only people here from your core are your parents. This is necessary because they must incarnate first. Since earthly time is moving fast, they will take over the bodies of other couples who are on the earthly plane. They will not have to relive their childhoods and courtship. They'll already be married and planning for your and Andrew's arrival, Angie. They will go through the veil of forgetfulness, so they'll have to understand the plan. Knowing the details will help them use their intuition to nudge their children in the right direction."

Angie noticed that her guardian angels had entered the room. "Hi, Arla, Reena, and Ed. I'm so happy to see you again. I promise I won't go over your heads directly to the archangels as I did."

Metatron piped up. "No worries Angie. We all work together, so call on any of us and the appropriate ones will help. You will have all fifteen archangels as your guardian angels as well as the three you already know and who are here now.

"You and Andrew will share the same eighteen guardian angels. Arla, Reena, and Ed are here to observe and learn the plan. You will often see sparkles of light in the colors you associate with the archangels along with white sparkles from Arla, Reena, and Ed. They will always be with you, so you will feel a peace come over you to let you know they are with you when you reach out to them. They will give you advice and help things come to pass by nudging them along. They will keep the ego-based thoughts of fear, insecurity, and anger suppressed."

Angie was grateful and squeezed Andrew's hand.

Raziel said, "The first decision to be made is when Angie and Andrew should arrive on Earth. Children don't have reasoning power until age seven. That would be a perfect time for them to walk in. They will find a couple of souls who would like to act as their placeholders and enrich their own karma until age seven. That will give Angie and Andrew more time to observe what is happening on the old Earth and find the loving souls.

"Angie and Andrew will often work closely together and therefore have already been granted the four gifts of clear seeing, feeling, thinking, and hearing. They will be sensitive children with psychic abilities. Though they will have to go through the veil of forgetfulness to enter the earthly place, the veil will be lifted immediately upon their entry. They will always remember what their mission is. They will communicate with their band of angels and the ETs. These gifts along with their intuition and sixth sense will overshadow their egos and free wills and will guide them to make all the correct, predetermined life choices.

"Angie, it's time for you and Andrew to make some choices. I know you have already selected December the eleventh for your birth date. Andrew's birth date will be June the twelfth. The Gemini-Sagittarian compatibility worked for you in your previous incarnations. Your parents have requested the same birthdays as they had for their last incarnations. A comfortable, middle-class upbringing will best suit your mission."

Raphael entered and said, "Angie, remember that when I need your attention, I might make books jump off their shelves, or I might drop one in front of you. It might startle you, but then you will remember."

Jophiel entered. "Angie, I promised to assist you with your wardrobe to help you achieve a look of respectful beauty. I'll also help you find an alarm clock that sounds like wind chimes to remind you of waking up in heaven."

Angie smiled at that wonderful thought.

Metatron said, "I have a suggestion that will make Angie and Andrew twice as powerful. Angie will still be in charge with Andrew by her side, but what about if they were both born as twins. I thought of this before but couldn't say anything until I thoroughly researched the idea. I feel two souls are ideally suited—Mary and Matthew. They have been soul mates through many lifetimes. I'd like them to join us before we discuss this further. Mary and Matthew, will you join us now?"

They entered the room and said hello to everyone. Mary spoke. "We've reviewed your plan to help shift the loving souls to the new Earth. The ruination of the old Earth disgusts us. We want to help. Metatron reviewed our akashic records and our cords in the tapestry of life. He showed us Angie's and Andrew's cords and records. We're very compatible. We want to help and are willing to join you as your twins if you'll have us. We will leave you now to discuss this. Metatron will let us know if you have more questions for us."

They left the room hand in hand.

Angie was the first to offer her thoughts. "This is a great idea. I'd like to have Mary as my twin. I think the girls will get to know each other and bond quicker if we have each other, and the same with the guys. I suggest they be granted the same psychic gifts as Andrew and I have been given along with the veil of forgetfulness being lifted after they enter. And one more thing—I'd like them to have the same eighteen guardian angels. This will make us a true foursome."

"I too believe they should have the same powers as Angie and Andrew have," Metatron said. "Twins have a way of communicating with each other that is on the verge of being psychic. They like the same things and complete each other's sentences and thoughts. No one would be the wiser if the twins possessed these additional gifts and psychic abilities. And that would double their powers. The girls will be twins as will the guys. They should not have any other siblings. Their parents will give their undivided attention to their twins and their mission. Yes, they should have the same eighteen guardian angels. But this will need approval of the Creator and the other archangels."

No sooner had Metatron made the statement than he had his answer. "We've received a resounding approval from the collective consciousness. Are there any more questions or concerns?" He paused. Everyone remained silent. Hearing nothing, he said, "I suggest we invite Mary and Matthew back to share the news and include them as we plan."

Angie remembered that Metatron would have also been with the Creator and the other archangels. She should not have been surprised at the immediate response.

Mary and Matthew joined them; the future twins enjoyed a group hug. They would need to get to know each other better; their spirits had to meld so they could recognize each other on the earthly and physical planes. Without a word, they scanned each other's minds and instantly understood they were destined to make the journey together, be together, and work together. They would be identical twins and alike in all ways.

Metatron said, "Angie, Andrew, Mary, and Matthew will all walk in at age seven, the guys in June and the girls in December of that year. The placeholders will meet each other as toddlers and become inseparable. They will attend the same schools and live in the same neighborhood. In adulthood, they will marry the other twins and will live together. Twins falling in love with twins will be accepted. It will keep them together and working together."

Raziel said, "I look forward to many dream-time visits from all of you to review your life's purpose, accomplishments, and goals. You will remember your dream-time visits distinctly as if they occurred during your waking hours. I agree with Metatron and would like to add that it is not important that you attend college. You need to get on with your mission. You'll have the best teachers in the galaxy."

Ariel stopped by and said, "They'll live together in a large home surrounded by fields of flowers full of birds and butterflies. Their home will reflect their love for each other and for the entire world to see. They'll need this refuge as an escape from the rigors of daily life and as a place to come together in peace and love. Their home will serve as a home for the fairies to gather in preparation for the shift. The details of how they will help the loving souls make the shift will be worked out."

The four had bonded and knew the basics of their earthly lives together; they couldn't have been happier. Angie and Andrew had been together since the beginning of time and would expand to an awesome foursome.

Archangel Jophiel joined them again. "It's time to enjoy one more gathering of friends and family before the parents of the group start incarnating to the earthly plane. Remember that nature renews your spirits and revives your energy levels. You will all need high energy as you start your mission. To celebrate your newfound friendship and bond more, you are invited to enjoy another banquet in the great outdoors with the beauty of nature reviving your souls. Spend time with your friends and relatives many of whom will be returning to the physical plane to begin their roles in the group incarnation."

Without another thought, they were at the banquet. It was as beautiful as Angie remembered. The unicorns romped in fields of flowers that stretched as far as they could see. The babbling brook looked so inviting that she wanted to dip her toes in it. The smell of the flowers tickled her nose. The double rainbows were a vision. This was the most gorgeous of all outdoor spaces; it was her hope for the new Earth. The night was theirs with no worries, cares, or concerns for what lay ahead. They danced, ate, and enjoyed each other's company well into the night. Time seemed to stand still as it always did in the spirit world. They did not have to worry about getting a good's night sleep the way they must sleep on Earth.

CHAPTER 29

General Council and back to Earth Featuring Archangels Metatron, Raguel, and Michael

After the delightful gathering, Jophiel appeared and said, "I am here to return you to the Processing Center. Metatron and Raguel will escort you to a meeting with the general council. Remember my promise to you, Angie, which I extend to Mary, Andrew, and Matthew. I will help beautify your thoughts and clothing choices."

They were all back in the Processing Center. Jophiel gave them all archangel hugs and angel blessings, and they watched her beautiful pink aura vanish into the distance.

Metatron said, "The general council is both the name of a special area as well as the name of the group that will bestow their final blessings on the plans for the mass incarnation. It's like a waiting room before you board an airplane for your return trip to Earth."

The area was not grandiose as the other areas they had visited; it was even more elegant. Against a backdrop of gold draperies were gorgeous fluted white columns that encircled the perimeter. Bright stars bathed in pale blue illuminated the interior. Angie's core group took their places on the lower tiers that resembled theater seats rising from the ornate white and gold podium. Behind them were hundreds of souls who represented the mass incarnation. Beautiful white furniture with curved designs trimmed in gold and arranged in the center denoted a place for the general council. At the sight of the podium, Angie was concerned she would be asked to address the council, but Metatron and Raguel assured her she had nothing to fear.

The council was ready. Seated in the place of prominence was Archangel Michael. Arla, Reena, and Ed were next to him, and Legna was on the other side. Behind them in a magnificent row were the other fourteen archangels Angie had met. They were a glorious sight; their individual colors radiated in the blue hue. Angie looked from one to another acknowledging and thanking them with her thoughts. She felt a common bond of love and appreciation with them all. It was surely as close to heaven as anyone could get unless he or she got the chance to meet the Creator as she had.

Michael spoke to the group with a loving but authoritative tone. "Normally, a council of angels handles the duties of the general council. Due to the seriousness of this mission, I will preside with the archangels as the messengers of the Creator. Let's begin."

Michael stepped back as Metatron came up to the podium and announced, "The Creator has reviewed the plans and agrees with all the details. Alterations can be worked out as needed. It's time for the parents to take the places of the souls who have been representing them on the earthly plane. The exchange will take place during sleeping hours when the placeholders will be summoned to the astral plane. The parents will take their places and awaken to a new day on Earth. They have been observing their placeholders from above, so the transition should be flawless with perhaps a few minor differences. They will bring the placeholder twins into the world. Mary and Matthew have spent time with their parents-to-be and have developed bonds and loving relationships. Everything should work out quite well.

"Angie, Andrew, Mary, and Matthew will make the exchange with their placeholders when they are seven. While they are here on the astral plane, they will carefully monitor what is going on in their families and with the loving souls. The foursome will play a very important part with the final shifting of all loving souls. We will discuss those details when the time is near. While you are here observing, your band of angels and the ETs will be here to help you."

Michael said, "The Creator offers his congratulations to all of you for this well-thought-out plan and asks you to go in love and peace."

Raguel stepped forward. "I will harmonize all relationships and bring orderliness, fairness, harmony, and justice along with forgiveness, peace, and calm. I will confer with everyone to make sure all concerns are dealt with and communicated throughout the core group and band of angels."

Michael ended the meeting. "I look forward to the day the mission is successfully completed and we meet here to celebrate a job well done. Until then, I send you all angel blessings."

The general council disbanded. The archangels gave archangel hugs to all and then departed; their auras faded into the distance. The core group also exchanged hugs and best wishes. The parents said their farewells as they left. The plan was in motion.

The seven years passed quickly. Angie, Andrew, Mary, and Matthew spent a lot of time in the Tapestry Room checking the brightness and density of the strands of the core group. They kept a close watch on the akashic record book. They observed and learned in the Library of Knowledge and School of Wisdom. They had a private observation deck to the earthly plane and memorized every aspect of the lives they would take over. At times, they were called upon to meet departed loved ones and help them cross over. When the souls from their extended group incarnated, they went to the Processing Center to see them off and wish them well.

After working hard and keeping extremely busy, they looked forward to free time in the meet-and-greet area when the four of them could be together enjoying nature to renew their spirits and revive their energy levels. They had frequent meetings with the archangels. Angie remained humble but was no longer awestruck at the sight of them. The feeling of love that radiated from them was beyond compare.

Before long, it was time for Andrew and Matthew to walk in. They coupled with their partners for one last time and immensely enjoyed each other. That delightful sensation would have to last until they met during dream times when their souls were ageless.

That night, the souls taking Andrew's and Matthew's places on Earth met with them, and their spirits intertwined. That coupling was very different from the coupling with their soul mates; it was for knowledge's sake only.

Angie and Mary accompanied Andrew and Matthew to the Processing Center. All fifteen archangels along with Arla, Reena, and Ed met them there. Sincere, loving hugs including archangel hugs were exchanged. Angel blessings and well wishes rang out, and then they were gone. They would wake up in their beds on the earthly plane. Azrael would escort their placeholders to heaven to help them cross over. They would walk in on their seventh birthdays to gifts and celebrations. There was talk that they would receive new bikes as birthday gifts.

Angie and Mary would watch from above wishing they could be there too, but they were very happy that the next phase of the plan had begun. However, they were sad and missed Andrew and Matthew every minute. Dream times were frequent and cherished when their spirits united in loving and compassionate coupling.

The six months of earth time flew by. It was time for Angie and Mary to walk in. They reviewed the plan with Metatron, who told them, "During dream time, the souls holding your places on the earthly plane will meet with you. Your spirits will intertwine, and knowledge will be exchanged. Angie and Mary, you will wake up in your beds on the earthly plane the next morning. Azrael will escort your placeholders and help them cross over. The exchange will be completed. The next phase of the plan will begin."

Angie and Mary were exhilarated. The veil of forgetfulness would be lifted as soon as they arrived on Earth; they would remember everything. Angie was determined to save the loving souls who deserved to move to the new Earth. She hoped that someday, they all would experience what she had experienced—an audience with the Creator along with the archangels amid the backdrop of all the twinkling stars and the souls that composed the universe—an extraordinary honor.

That night, Angie and Mary reviewed the first seven years of their placeholders' time on Earth so all memories would be vivid in their minds as they walked in to begin their lives on the earthly plane.

PART III

Life back on Earth

CHAPTER 30

Happy Birthday Featuring Archangels Michael, Raphael, and Gabriel

Angie and Mary watched their birth and early years from above. Even the minutest detail was imprinted in their minds and souls as if they had experienced everything firsthand.

They witnessed the night preceding their birth. It was a night out of a horror film. A hard rain pelted the windows, and the winds blew so hard that the tree limbs were creaking. The lights flickered. Their father tried to comfort their mother. He knew in his heart it was time for his girls to be born, but he wondered how he would get his wife to the hospital. He had no training or experience to handle one birth let alone two. His silent prayer to the Lord was to keep his daughters safe. *Please Lord, please*, he begged as the house was plunged into darkness.

His wife let out a scream. Labor had begun. Angie and Mary saw how worried their parents were. The roads were slippery and treacherous. Their parents silently asked Archangel Michael to keep all four of them safe and protect their vehicle and all the vehicles around them. They asked Archangel Raphael to take care of them all and to bring their daughters safely into the world.

Angie and Mary wished they could have let them know everything would be fine. It had to be. That was part of the plan, and the archangels would make sure they were all safe.

The overnight bag had been packed and ready for weeks. Their dad grabbed their mom's raincoat and slid it over her shoulders. They heard him whisper in a brave voice, "It's time. All will be well.

The angels are watching over us." They wondered if their dad was recalling the plan and the band of angels.

With bag and keys in hand, he guided their mom out the front door and into the brutal night. He got her into the car despite the rain-soaked driveway and strong winds. He hurried to get behind the wheel. Angie and Mary heard his silent prayer of thanks and his request that Archangels Michael and Raphael keep them safe. He tried not to show any concern as the car engine sputtered and then sputtered again. After another pleading prayer, the car started. He eased out of the driveway. Tree limbs littered the road, and debris was flying. The roads were slick, and it was hard for him to see the occasional car that passed them. It was unusual weather for that time of year.

They drove in silence except for her occasional gasp as her labor pains intensified. Angie and Mary heard his constant prayers to the angels. The girls asked the angels to put their parents at ease and felt the immediate answer to their request as a calmness came over them while they completed their journey on that treacherous night. They arrived at the emergency room and did not have to beckon anyone—a wheelchair appeared at their mom's door, and she was whisked inside. Angie and Mary had made sure of that.

Their dad parked the car and raced back to the hospital. He ran down the hallway asking for directions as he flew by the reception area. Their mom was already in a hospital gown; she'd shed her rain-soaked garments that must have given her and her babies a chill to their bones.

Nurses were helping with her panting and breathing while he shed his wet raincoat and joined her side. He thanked the Lord and Michael for getting them safely to the hospital. His focus shifted to Raphael and Gabriel. He asked them to assist with the safe delivery of his girls into the world. He asked that his girls be healthy. He helped their mom through the next contraction when the doctor arrived and told them it was time to move to the delivery room.

The screams of labor stopped. Sounds of babies crying shattered the momentary silence of the delivery room. The twins had arrived. Their mother looked exhausted. A peaceful smile crept over her face as she asked to hold her babies. Two beautiful baby girls were placed in her arms. As she snuggled them to her breast, she whispered, "Angie and Mary, our angels."

They looked identical except for the colored ribbons on their ankles; Angie's was white and Mary's was pink. From above, Angie and Mary had nudged the nurses to make sure they got the names correct and that the ribbons correctly identified them. Everything was going according to plan.

A couple of weeks later, their parents conveyed their total happiness as they shared their first Christmas with their newborns. They dressed them alike in outfits that made them look like cherubs. They wore caps to keep them cozy and warm. Angie's was white and Mary's was pink. Those were their identification colors, but their parents knew who they were by instinct. It was a merry Christmas.

Angie and Mary enjoyed recalling their birth and reminiscing about the early years. They were mirror images. They watched their other selves as they learned how to talk, walk, feed themselves, and soak up knowledge. Their accomplishments were always at the same time. They had even cut their first teeth on the same day. They were inseparable and loving and never upset with each other. If one cried, the other did too. It was a challenge for their parents, but they didn't mind.

Angie and Mary watched them start preschool and then kindergarten. Their knowledge was growing. They had loving parents and teachers, and everything had moved along as planned.

Angie and Mary's placeholders met Andrew and Matthew in preschool and formed an instant bond because they were all twins. They played together very well and never had an angry or upsetting thought between them.

After their parents met, they arranged play dates for their children. As the children bonded, so did their parents. Though the parents had gone through the veil of forgetfulness, they seemed to have an inner knowledge that they would all become loving friends. Angie and Mary had front-row seats for the first seven years of their lives. It came time for their walk in.

CHAPTER 31

Childhood—Gifted Children Featuring All Archangels

Angie and Mary spent their last day on the heavenly plane making final preparations. They checked the tapestry of life for any last-minute changes. The cords looked great. In the akashic record book, they scanned the names of key people in their core group including Andrew and Matthew not expecting to find problems. Fortunately, they didn't.

They took their posts on the observation deck and watched their earthbound placeholders. They had reviewed their birth and childhood and then closed their eyes for the night, their last night on the astral plane. It was almost time. Angie's thoughts wandered. Sleep was impossible with the excitement that was bubbling up in her. She snapped back to reality when Mary gave her a nudge.

There before them was Archangel Gabriel complete with his trumpet and with an army of angels behind him. She recognized all the archangels she had met on her heavenly journey. She saw Haniel, the moon; Raziel, the rainbow; Sandalphon, musical notes; Uriel, the sun; Michael, the mighty sword; and Metatron, the giant cube. Ariel looked like a pretty, pink princess. Even Azrael had taken time away from her grief counseling and crossing people over to be there to bid them farewell. Jeremiel was there with his gold shooting stars.

They saw another beautiful archangel with a leafy-green aura they had seen but not met. They found Jophiel in the group looking like a delicate porcelain doll. Raphael held the caduceus, the symbol of medicine, amid his sparkling green emeralds. Last but not least, she saw Zadkiel in his shades of purple that always reminded Angie of the colors associated with the crucifixion. They were all there along with their guardian angels Arla, Reena, and Ed.

Beyond those she recognized were angels as far as she could see. Row after row of angels were gently hovering against the backdrop of the starlit sky. It was a magnificent sight, a memory she would cherish. Angie and Mary looked at each other in astonishment. They could never remember seeing so many angels even during their stay on the heavenly plane.

Archangel Michael spoke. "Greetings to you, Angie and Mary. We are ready to escort you to your beds on the earthly plane. We have brought an army of angels. They were always around you but usually chose not to be seen. We want you to see them all and realize you have thousands of angels helping you. We will escort you to Earth and remain close. We will be visible only to both of you. We all pledge our love and support. We will be with you always. We bring reassurances from the Creator that your mission will be successful."

These messages had a profound effect on them. They had been extremely busy worrying about every detail of their mission, so this was a perfect reminder that they were loved and were partnered with the almighty Creator and his multitude of angels.

Angie and Mary held hands as they joined the archangels at the front of the mighty angelic parade that would guide them to the earthly plane that night. They glided effortlessly and soon found themselves resting comfortably in their beds. If only others could have seen the beautiful sight of an army of powerful, graceful angels floating through the air and hovering beside them.

Everything was going according to plan. No one besides Angie and Mary and their band of angels would know what had happened that night. Angie knew that there might be some differences their parents, relatives, and friends would notice between them and their placeholders. They had studied every intricate detail all of which were engraved in their souls' memories as if each experience had been their own.

There had been careful planning to find Angie and Mary a couple of souls who were just like them and who shared their personality traits and emotions. The girls thought it would be an easy transition. Before Angie and Mary drifted off to sleep, they saw their placeholders and waved goodbye as they floated heavenward accompanied by the Archangel Azrael, who would help them cross over. There would be no need for their placeholders to leave signs for their departed loved ones because they had just switched places. Instead, they would be attending a welcome-home party that night with their friends, loved ones, and soul mates in the meet-and-greet area.

Speaking of soul mates, Angie thought of Andrew while Mary thought of Matthew. They had been missing them so much and could hardly wait to meet up with them, but it was time to get some sleep. As they closed their eyes, the angels disappeared from view but not from their sides.

In no time at all, Angie and Mary woke up feeling totally refreshed and ready to get on with their mission. First, they had to adjust to the dense atmosphere of the earthly plane; the heavenly plane had been so light, airy, and effortless. They had been accustomed to floating and getting around by merely thinking where they wanted to be, but they would have to walk. They had been experts in communicating through thoughts, but they would have to talk and choose their words wisely.

Telepathic communication was great. Everyone knew what everyone else was thinking; everyone knew the entire story without verbal explanation. Walking, talking, communicating, and eating were activities they had not done since the last time they had been on the earthly plane. There was no need for food in heaven; it was there for souls to enjoy, but it was not necessary. Angie and Mary were communicating through their thoughts and knew what each other was thinking and feeling. It was easy for identical twins to share that trait, so no one would know they had been granted special gifts.

It was time to get out of bed, put their feet on the floor, and walk to the kitchen for breakfast and talk to their parents. Though their parents knew the plan, they would not remember the details, but they would have inclinations and be nudged by the angels.

Before they left their bedroom, Archangels Gabriel and Metatron appeared to them. Gabriel reminded the girls that they were children, not grown-ups, and must act that way. One of Gabriel's specialties was children, so he would be there to help with the transition.

Metatron had his cube and was there to observe and to make sure all the details of the plan worked out flawlessly. He also worked with special children, which they surely were.

Before they left, Metatron needed to clear their chakras. His clearing would not remove anything that was loved based. One by one, the cube moved down through the top of their heads and through their bodies. In no time at all, it was done. The archangels were ready to leave, but before they did, they gave the girls mighty archangel hugs.

The girls ran downstairs and realized they had conquered running as well as walking. Their parents wished them good morning and happy birthday. In their excitement, they had forgotten. Hugs and kisses were exchanged. The smells of breakfast tickled their noses. They were remembering to speak and found themselves communicating effortlessly. They were adjusting to the dense atmosphere of Earth quite nicely.

Their parents reminded them that it was Sunday and time to get ready for church. They quickly ran back upstairs to get washed and dressed. They hurried back downstairs, but breakfast was not quite ready. They had time to go outside and do a little exploring in the backyard. "We'll be out back!" they shouted as they flew out into the bright sunlight of a beautiful day. They recalled Archangel Ariel and the breathtaking places they had visited on the heavenly plane. Their backyard was not nearly as beautiful, but it would do. The lawn was nicely manicured and adorned with flowers and nice trees. They especially loved the screened-in porch and vowed to spend many a day and night out there looking toward the heavens. So far, the transition was working out just fine.

Bounding toward them from a corner of the yard was their Dalmatian, Wendy, the last dog Angie and Andrew owned during their previous incarnations. It was decided that Wendy would incarnate into their family to provide loving friendship for Angie and Mary. Wendy certainly remembered Angie and smothered her with kisses. Her tail was wagging so fast that it looked like it might fly off her body. Angie was happy to see her again. She wondered when Andrew would get to see her. She hoped it would be soon because she wanted to see him too. It was time to get back to exploring.

CHAPTER 32

Meeting the Fairies Featuring Archangel Ariel

Angie picked up a Mason jar that held a candle. As she admired the beautiful candle, the jar tumbled right out of her hands. "Oh no! I'll get in so much trouble. Maybe it could be glued back together," she cried out.

That was not how she had wanted her first day on the old Earth to start. The good news was that the candle was intact. Even the way the bottom of the jar had separated from the top was seamless. Mary was sympathetic. The perfectly round jar bottom was curious. Angie held it up to the sunlight, and it almost blinded her. As she took the glass away from her eyes, she thought she saw something. She looked through it again but was careful to direct her gaze away from the sun.

At first, everything looked normal. It was not a prescription glass like eyeglasses would have been. Nothing seemed to look farther away or closer or clearer. But she caught a glimpse of something— maybe an insect darting by. As she held up the glass disk again, she pretended it was a spyglass. She started scanning the bushes and flower beds. The flower petals almost seemed alive as the gentle breezes lifted and dropped them in a graceful, waving motion. The morning dew hadn't totally dried up in the rays of the sun. Dew glistened and twinkled everywhere. She handed the looking glass to Mary so she could see the beauty Angie was seeing.

Just then, they heard a call from the kitchen that breakfast was ready, so off they ran. Angie slipped the looking glass into her pocket.

They decided they would do more exploring later. They were starved at the thought of one of their mom's yummy Sunday breakfasts they had observed from above. Weekdays and even Saturday breakfasts were quick, but not Sunday breakfasts; their mom had more time then.

They washed their hands and sat down to a wonderful breakfast that included fresh, cut-up fruit that squished in their mouths and got rid of their nighttime cotton mouth. They enjoyed turkey bacon, sunny-side-up eggs, scrambled eggs, homemade biscuits, and blueberry pancakes. While they ate, they forgot all about the looking glass. After a delightful breakfast, they got freshened up for church. Angie and Mary discussed what it would be like attending Mass after they had lived on the astral plane and had met all the archangels.

They walked up the church steps with their parents and glanced at the statutes of Jesus and Mary in the lobby. They appeared to be looking directly at them. They glanced at each other as they thought they saw a twinkle in their eyes. Remembering some of the last words Jesus had said to them—"We will always be with you"—convinced them that the twinkle was real. They knew they didn't need to be in church to be with them, but it seemed they were receiving a special greeting. They decided that Mass would be extra special from then on. The statutes were perfect replicas of Jesus and Mary as they appeared in the heavenly plane.

As their thoughts wandered from the celebration of the Mass, they remembered the looking glass. Angie reached into her pocket and ran her fingers over the glass enjoying its smooth, sturdy feel. There were no rough edges, so their fingers would not be cut. She slipped it into Mary's pocket. It was fun reading each other's thoughts. They knew they were both anxious to look through it again. The church service was ending, and the parishioners started moving in their seats.

Back home, Dad was reading the newspaper and Mom was doing the laundry. The girls finished their chores and ran outside with Wendy. They played fetch with her favorite squeaky toy until she ran inside for some water and returned to plop down for a rest.

Angie and Mary had the backyard to themselves. Mary slipped the looking glass out of her pocket and started to survey the yard on that beautiful day. The backyard wonderland was alive with the excited cries of the hatchlings as blue jays, mockingbirds, and cardinals brought food to their young. Angie and Mary remembered when a blue jay nest had fallen out of the tree in their front yard. They watched their placeholders put the nest in a shoebox on top of a stepladder in their garage where they lovingly fed the baby birds. When they started to jump around the box, they put the stepladder outside. Much to their surprise and delight, the mother and father blue jays returned to teach their offspring to fly. The girls realized at the same time that they hadn't been there. They had observed that event from above, and it was ingrained in their memories as if they had experienced it firsthand. This was another indication that their transition was working perfectly.

A black and yellow butterfly was darting around Angie's head. Mom had always said that was a sign that someone was sending a hello from heaven. They wondered who.

Mary handed the lens to Angie, who surveyed the yard and saw something incredible—fairies curled up sleeping. "Mary, look! Fairies are sleeping in the petals of the flowers!"

Mary took the looking glass and squealed in delight, "I see them!"

"Hush," whispered Angie. "We don't anyone to know our secret. When I visited the fairies with Ariel, she explained that they slept in the day and partied all night. We'll have to come back tonight to see them dance. They love to dance. Wait until you see them!"

A call from the house broke the spell. Angie slipped the looking glass, a treasure providing a glimpse into another world, into her pocket, and called to Wendy. They ran into the house to see what their mom wanted. She was going to the gardening store and wanted them to come.

"Can we plant some things in the backyard?" the girls asked in unison. The minute their mom assured them they could, they piled into the car.

The garden shop was a magical place with all sorts of colors and fragrances. They wanted one of everything. Angie felt the looking glass in her pocket. They found a quiet area in the garden shop by the tools where they still had full view of the plants. They took turns looking through the lens and saw fairies everywhere. Most appeared to be sleeping under the leaves of the plants. A few were drinking the nectar of the flowers as if waking up for a nighttime glass of water.

It was a glorious sight. They wished the garden shop were open at night. They were sure it would be a true fairyland then. Their mom had the plants and flowers selected and paid for. It was time to go home.

As soon as they got home, they put on gardening gloves, grabbed some tools, and started to plant their purchases. Their mom knew exactly where each one should go. The birds were chirping, and butterflies were flitting around. Whenever a butterfly came by, the girls would say hello to it in unison.

The plants were soon settled in their new homes and watered, and the tools were cleaned up. They washed their hands and returned to the backyard with some refreshing lemonade. As they glided on the porch swing, they took out their looking glass expecting to see the fairies still asleep.

But the fairies were gone. Sadness washed over them. They took turns looking closer and saw that they had gathered. Something was going on. They looked closer and saw a fairy seemingly entangled in a weed vine that grew like a blanket over the jasmine.

The girls wanted to help the fairy. As they moved closer watching through the looking glass, the other fairies scattered. They had to help the one who was stuck. Angie spoke softly while Mary ran to grab the pruners. Mary carefully made a couple of snips several inches around the fairy, but still no movement. She made a couple of more snips and then carefully wiggled the vines to let the fairy know they were loose. They moved away very slowly, and the other fairies reassembled. With their wings beating rapidly, the fairies gingerly lifted their friend and carried her away.

"Where did they go? Was the fairy injured? Was she exhausted from the struggle? Will we recognize that fairy again? She had had a yellow pinafore with a yellow sash around the waist. Do they all dress differently? Will they understand we had helped them? Do they realize we saw them?" The girls had so many questions. They called to Archangel Ariel to help the injured fairy. Angie remembered Ariel had told her she would be given a way to see the fairies. The broken jar had not been an accident after all—it was a looking glass from Ariel.

Time flew by that afternoon. It was time for dinner. They heard their mom call out to them. She thanked them for helping with the gardening and reminded them to wash up for dinner.

The girls were pleasantly surprised when they returned to the dinner table and saw balloons and gifts. Merriment filled the air. They finished dinner quickly so they could get to their dessert—a delicious chocolate cake. Seven candles burned brightly as their parents sang "Happy Birthday." Angie and Mary held hands, silently made the same wish, and blew out the candles. They unwrapped their gifts of matching dolls and doll clothes.

With lots of love and laughter in the air, the girls asked if they could take Wendy out before they headed to bed. Out the door they ran with their looking glass in hand. Right before their eyes was a playful group of fairies jumping from leaf to leaf along the jasmine hedge. Overjoyed, Angie gave Mary the lens; she couldn't speak. All she could do was point to the area where she had seen them. She could tell by Mary's surprised look that she saw them too. They saw fairies smelling the tiny, fragrant flowers of the hedge while others were darting around in a happy-go-lucky manner. The fairies had no idea they were being watched. They danced in fairy circles and left what seemed to be trails of fairy dust behind them on the wind. Angie and Mary didn't see the injured fairy and hoped she was okay.

The girls wanted to stay there all night, but soon, their parents called them in. It was time for bed, and they needed to sleep. They had had such a full day, and they were anxious to see Andrew and Matthew at school the following day.

The next morning before they headed off to school, they heard faint bells in their backyard. They scampered out to investigate but could not find anything until they looked through their looking glass. The fairies were back, and they were ringing their bells and jumping up and down. "They must have figured out we could see them and knew how to get our attention. The fairy in the yellow pinafore is jumping all over and ringing her bell the loudest. They know we helped her, and they're letting us know she's all right," Angie told Mary.

The girls gave a little wave, and to their surprise, all the fairies waved back as they settled into their leaves and petals for their daytime sleep. There was no doubt that Ariel had helped. Angie and Mary ran inside to catch their ride to school; they were anxious to see Andrew and Matthew for the first time.

CHAPTER 33

Coming of Age Featuring Archangels Ariel and Metatron

The moment they saw the girls, Andrew and Matthew knew that their soul mates, the authentic Angie and Mary, had arrived on the earthly plane. No one else could understand why they were so happy that day.

At lunchtime, the girls told the guys about the looking glass and the injured fairy. They couldn't wait to show them. The best time would be at night, but unfortunately, that was a school night. But Mary had overheard their moms talking about getting together on Friday night. It was agreed—Andrew and Matthew would come over to see the fairies on Friday night.

The home life and school life transitions had been effortless. Finally, Friday night arrived. Angie, Mary, Andrew, and Matthew were on the back patio talking and waiting for the sun to go down. Angie slipped the looking glass out of her pocket, took the first look, and spotted the fairies. Mary peeked next and pointed out a good spot for Andrew and Matthew to look at. The guys were surprised that they could see them too.

As nightfall approached, the fairies were yawning and stretching as they woke up to enjoy the evening. The fairies thanked Angie and Mary for saving their friend, whom they called Sunshine. They explained that Ariel had brought them there to their temporary home and that more would be coming while they waited to go to their new home. They were so delicate; Ariel wanted them to receive love and special protection during the waiting period.

Moonlight broke through the clouds and cast moonbeams around the backyard. Angie sent a hello up to Archangel Haniel. The fairies were holding hands and dancing around in circles in the garden. They looked so happy. There was Sunshine dancing with them as if nothing had happened to her.

When Angie wondered how the fairies stayed safe from danger and the neighborhood cats, Archangel Ariel appeared to explain. "First, thank you for calling on me to help Sunshine. She's fine as you can see. In fairyland, they use the toad-warning system. If a cat is prowling around at night while the fairies are preoccupied with their parties, the toads send out a warning signal to the cats. Cats do not like toads that can shoot poison in their mouths if they don't behave. The fairies take turns standing guard during the day. Many more fairies will be arriving here in preparation for the shift."

Angie stated, "We love them! Send them all to us. We will take care of them as best we can. If we need your help, we'll call you!"

The years flew by. The four were inseparable. The looking glass remained their secret. Whenever they had the time, they sat outside and watched the fairies for hours especially on nights of the full moon. Their numbers grew and grew until the backyard was teeming with delightful fairies dancing all night and sleeping in flower petals during the day.

During dream time, Angie, Mary, Andrew, and Matthew would often meet on the heavenly plane where they were all grown up despite their younger ages on Earth. They thoroughly enjoyed coupling when they would intermingle their spirits to forge stronger bonds. The archangels and Legna expressed approval of their earthly progress but at the same time expressed concern that the old Earth was very close to total annihilation.

During one dream time, Legna explained, "All the ETs are working very diligently to slow down the inevitable. They can't interfere with a soul's free will. They are capable of other means to stall the old Earth's inescapable demise. If they must, they can disarm nuclear bombs and cause earthquakes, hurricanes, and all other types of natural disasters. They don't like to do that because many innocent souls could be hurt and could lose their lives, homes, and livelihoods, but sometimes, they have no choice. We can always count on the good souls to unite to help their fellowman.

"Undoubtedly, the negative souls will greedily analyze the situation to increase their own personal wealth. The ETs have a very important role in the development of the new Earth as well. They hardly have any time to meet with you because of their monumental tasks. That will change after the shift, when you will be in constant contact with them. For now, it is time for me to say goodbye."

Driver's licenses and voter registration cards were signs that they were coming of age and getting closer to their life's purpose—the shift. Archangel Michael was called upon to keep them safe behind the wheel along with Archangel Gabriel, the patron saint of travel. Their parents did not challenge them when they announced they would not be going to college but would get jobs instead. There was no need for higher education when they had access to all the knowledge they needed in the universal Library of Knowledge. Their professors were the angels and archangels under the guidance of the Creator. Their time on that planet was better spent in preparation for the shift. And time was running out.

One night during dream time, Angie, Mary, Andrew, and Matthew were summoned by Archangel Metatron for a special meeting to plan their future. They met in the magnificent library where the spirit guide directed them to a quiet area. Metatron greeted them with archangel hugs, always a delight for Angie.

Metatron started the meeting with a question. "Angie, do you remember the first time you were told that you were selected to lead a very important mission?"

"I sure do, and I remember asking, 'Why me?' I thought someone like the pope or a winner of the Nobel Peace Prize would be more deserving. I was told that you needed someone who had love in her heart and that I did through many incarnations."

"Correct!" responded Metatron. "And now it's time to explain how we need your assistance. How will the four of you help the loving souls get ready for the shift? First, let me explain vibrations. You understand that there are many levels of vibrations on the astral plane. You have experienced the lowest, and you were given the opportunity to meet the Creator, where you experienced the highest vibration possible if only for a moment.

"There are different vibrational levels among the planets. The new Earth will have a higher vibration than the old Earth has. Before the loving souls can shift, they must be taught how to raise their vibrations. That will allow them to communicate with the universe and the Creator, angels, and ETs after the shift. The four of you have experienced the higher vibration on the astral plane and will take that remembrance and vibration with you."

Angie respectfully and sheepishly asked, "Why can't the angels or Creator raise everyone's vibrational level?"

Metatron responded. "Angie, you always have such good questions, and that one is the basis of our need for your help. Angels and those on the astral plane cannot do this because of free will. We need an incarnated, earth-dwelling soul to teach the loving souls how to achieve the higher vibration. You need to encourage them, and in turn, they'll encourage others. Eventually, the free-will choice to raise their vibrations will be accepted by the loving souls worldwide.

"That will be your vocation, all four of you. We will work with you to teach the souls, and we need you to teach as many as quickly as possible. The best way to accomplish this is to start an internet school with video classes. You will travel and hold conferences and make guest appearances for others."

"That sounds wonderful," Angie said. "But teaching loving souls to be better loving souls? How do we accomplish that? How can you teach others to raise their vibration?"

Metatron responded. "Angie, those are more very good questions. The simple answer is with the help of the archangels of course. To break it down further, three components are necessary to raise a soul's vibration—meditation, universal knowledge, and acceptance of the angels. I'm aware that all of you practice meditation every day and have been doing so for years. You know how to quiet your minds to reach that peaceful place. You know how to coordinate your breaths while raising your vibrations higher and higher with each inhale.

"Many loving souls already practice meditation but may not be fully reaping the benefits after quieting their minds. Experts in this field will assist you, and one well-known teacher of meditation that comes to mind is Manny."

"We know Manny," Angie said. "We've watched his videos and taken his classes, and we follow his practices. He taught us the techniques. It would be awesome if he could help us teach others. We could use his videos as teaching guides. He could be a guest speaker at conferences." Angie saw the others nodding.

Metatron said, "Then that component is settled. I'll ask Manny to join us during dream time and meet with you on the earthly plane. The next component is universal knowledge—the understanding of the universe and our Creator. Individualism has left many feeling that they are all alone in the world. During a crisis, they pray but are not sure whom they're asking for help. Angie, you had firsthand experience with universal knowledge when you met the Creator. We need you to share your knowledge with others so they will understand they are part of something much more wonderful and magical."

"How can I make people understand when they haven't experienced what I have?" Angie asked. "I wish I could bring everyone to meet the Creator, but I know that's not possible. And I know they don't remember because of the veil of forgetfulness."

Metatron calmed her fears. "There is an expert teacher of the concept of the universe. Cosmo has a huge following and has a special gift that makes people stop, think, and realize they are not mere specks on the planet but are part of the never-ending universe. You are correct that the veil of forgetfulness clouds this important fact, but Cosmo helps them remember."

"We follow him on social media, have taken his classes, and have attended his conferences," Angie said. "He's a perfect choice, and he can help us teach others. Please have him meet us here too."

"I know you are familiar with both Manny and Cosmo, and that is why they fit in perfectly with the plan," Metatron said. "Now let's talk about angels. On the new Earth, the loving souls will become skilled in the art of communication with the angels. Some may even see them when the angels wish to be seen. But before they can communicate with the angels, they must believe in them. The four of you have interacted with at least fifteen of the many archangels. As witnesses who have the gift of remembrance, you will bring your enthusiasm to others, and you will have help."

Before he could offer a name, Angie blurted out, "Casey! Yes, we love him too. Casey talks about the angels in such a way that you can feel their presence. His following talks about their angels as if they remember them. Please ask these experts to visit us during dream time. How do we begin? This is so exciting!"

Metatron explained. "As part of my research, I've already reached out to Manny, Cosmo, and Casey. The archangels met with them during dream time and explained the shift and the importance of your mission. They understood and feel privileged to be included. They have promised to keep their knowledge of the shift confidential. They know that if word got out, the negative souls would panic and go to extraordinary and unscrupulous means to be included.

"Now you have the foundation—the teachers in your internet school. Loving souls will be attracted to the concept and anxious to learn. You will hold seminars, and these experts will be your speakers. I've saved the best for last. Every business must have a special name. The name of your school will be Loving Vibrations, a perfect name for loving souls to learn how to raise their vibrations."

"Metatron, you have come up with a wonderful plan with great support to back us," Angie said enthusiastically. "The name Loving Vibrations is perfect. We're ready, right, guys?"

The others nodded.

"There's no time to waste," Metatron said. "The school must be available immediately. Your guest appearance and conference tour schedules will be grueling but necessary. The four of you must raise the vibration of every loving soul. Until that's done, the shift is on hold."

Archangel Michael entered the room. "It's time for me to bestow a blessing on you that will allow you to easily see the vibrations of all souls on Earth. Those with the brightest auras have raised their vibrations, but those with lesser vibrancy need your help. The dark vibrations are to be ignored. Peace be with you as you complete your mission."

And then he was gone.

Metatron gave them archangel hugs. "It's time for you to return to your beds on Earth. I'll continue to work out the details for you."

The next morning, they woke up anxious to discuss Loving Vibrations and agreed to meet over breakfast.

CHAPTER 34

Loving Vibrations Featuring Archangels Metatron, Michael, and Gabriel

The following night, they were again summoned by Metatron and fully expected to be discussing Loving Vibrations and perhaps meeting with Manny, Cosmo, and Casey. But Metatron had a different order for their priorities.

"I've called you here tonight because you need a home. You want to move out on your own, get married, and live together. We, speaking on behalf of the archangels, agree, and once again, I've done some research. A beautiful home has been on the market for quite some time. The owner hasn't been able to sell it, but I've come up with a plan for you to rent it and eventually purchase it. This home will stay in your family even after the shift. It will be home for many generations to come."

The foursome responded, "That sounds great! When can we see it? When can we move in? Aren't we going to get married first? Don't we need to get Loving Vibrations going first?"

Metatron calmed them down. "First things first. Yes, we need to get all the aspects of Loving Vibrations underway quickly for the shift but also so you can earn money to afford a home. And then there are the weddings. Wedding planning can be time consuming, so we will ask the archangels to handle that for you. Don't worry. They know you all very well and will make choices they are sure you will love. Let's get back to Loving Vibrations. I have asked some archangels and special guests to join us."

Angie was bubbling over at thoughts of a wedding and home, but she was also very anxious to see the archangels again and meet the special guests.

Archangel Michael joined them. "Hello, my dear ones. It's great to see you all again. Metatron has filled me in on his research. Loving Vibrations is perfect for the mission and for all of you. I will protect you and your business from all negative outside influences. I will also help put together the website with Archangel Gabriel."

Gabriel entered and greeted them. "Hello, hello. I too love the plans Metatron has come up with. Michael will make sure Loving Vibrations represents the highest possible spiritual path with the utmost integrity. I offer my expertise as your leader. As the archangel of communications, I will assist with the website and with all aspects of communicating love to your following. Metatron will continue to organize, research, and set priorities. Before we continue, I'll invite our special guests to join us."

Manny entered the meeting first. "I'm honored to be part of your very important mission. With the planet in disarray, the loving souls need to reduce their stress as they raise their vibrations. They need to incorporate meditation into their daily practice, not just when panic sets in. By the time they get to the new Earth, they will realize the value of continuing this practice. I have hundreds of recordings and videos that will be helpful.

"Let me lead you in a five-minute meditation. We will use the chant *aum* as the affirmation that the divine presence is the universe. Please close your eyes. Take three deep breaths. With each inhale, feel your body relax and your vibration physically rise higher and higher in you. As you continue to breathe, remember to push away any thoughts that enter your mind and refocus. Connect to the peacefulness, and you will communicate with the Creator."

They followed his instructions and soon heard him say, "When you're ready, open your eyes."

Metatron thanked Manny and invited him to stay while they welcomed the other special guests. Unbeknown to everyone, Cosmo had joined them and had participated in the meditation.

Cosmo said, "Hello fellow members of the universe. I am Cosmo, and I am ecstatic to be included in your extremely important mission. I have spread the message that we are all part of the universe.

Unfortunately, negativity is spreading over the planet. A new planet filled with loving souls without any negative free will and with everyone remembering their life's purpose is beyond my wildest hopes. I will encourage my tribe to follow Loving Vibrations, and I look forward to doing seminars and conferences with you. Metatron, excellent idea! I understand we cannot share the plans of the mission with anyone at this time, but I want to help in any way I can. Thank you again."

Casey had joined them as they were listening to Cosmo and announced his presence. "I am Casey, and I am all about angels and archangels. I want to help all people understand and appreciate their angels. Guardian angels be ready. You have been standing by, but now, you will be called upon.

"And thank you, Mother Earth. We have tried to get the population to take care of you and thank and appreciate you. Many do, but many more take you for granted and even more do not protect you. The plans for Mother Earth to shift to the new planet Earth are spectacular. The loving souls are deserving. A place where souls will meditate, connect with the universe, and communicate with their angels is heaven on earth. Count me in."

Archangel Metatron thanked them all. "Your participation in this very important mission is essential. We will work with you individually on your components. Archangel Jeremiel will help with a smooth and harmonious transition and will assist Manny with the meditation component. You can't have a school without tests. Archangels Zadkiel and Uriel will help the students remember the information and facts. With their assistance as well as guidance from Archangel Gabriel, all students will find that they can pass the tests as they become skilled in writing and speaking to spread the word.

"Archangel Raguel will work his magic and attract new students. Jophiel will help me with the organization and utilize her expertise at decluttering resulting in a smoothly run school. Chamuel will help coordinate all aspects of your homes and the jobs so you won't become burdened with the demands on your lives. And of course let's not forget the ETs. Legna has offered their support even though they are extremely busy right now."

Archangel and group hugs were exchanged as they departed their dream time to return to their earthly beds.

In no time at all, Loving Vibrations was ready. The enrollment in their internet school had exceeded their wildest expectations. They had numerous conferences scheduled throughout the United States. Their passports were ready as they discussed taking their message around the world. The assistance they received from Manny, Cosmo, and Casey had been phenomenal. The foursome had grown to seven as they became the best of friends and associates. With their band of archangels and angels, they were unstoppable.

They had a conference scheduled in Hawaii, and Metatron had another idea, so he called another meeting. "Hello, my hard workers. Your success is evident. We are all hopeful for the future. Your wedding plans are ready, and a date has been set. What about traveling to Hawaii after your wedding, attending the conference, and staying for your honeymoon? That will give you some time to rest before you take up your breakneck pace again. Cosmo, Manny, and Casey have agreed to keep things moving in your absence. Of course, the archangels will watch over Loving Vibrations too."

Angie and Mary spoke in unison. "We love the idea! What about our house? Can we move in after the wedding and honeymoon?"

Metatron gave them archangel hugs and assured them their home was in his plans too.

CHAPTER 35

United in Love Featuring Many Archangels

With nudging from the archangels, both sets of parents had planned an elaborate wedding. The twins' favorite colors that matched the ribbons on their ankles at birth were highlighted—Angie's was white, Mary's was pink, Andrew's was blue, and Matthew's was green.

Their wedding day arrived. Jophiel's promise to help them beautify themselves was exemplified in her choice of their wedding gowns. They were dressed alike with one small exception—Angie's garter was white while Mary's was pink—but no one would know that until the guys removed the garters at the reception.

They wondered if their friends and relatives would be able to tell them apart. Their gowns were pure white overlaid with lace on a fabric that gently swayed as they walked. Their veils were very elegant with long trains that flowed behind them. The girls looked like angels without wings—very befitting.

Archangel Ariel had handled all the flower arrangements. Angie's favorite gardenias and Mary's favorite pink tea roses were in bouquets that cascaded gracefully down from their hands. They were ready. They drove to the church in a limo they knew had been arranged by Archangel Michael because they caught a glimpse of him standing by the open door.

They carefully walked up the steps to the church as they had done many Sundays before, but this time was different—so special. They were anxious to see Andrew and Matthew. They looked in the church and saw their grooms standing on the altar in their white tuxes. Andrew had a blue boutonniere, and Matthew had a green one. White lilies decorated the altar, and pink lilies marked the pews. The girls sent up a thank-you to Ariel. Everything was picturesque.

As they got ready to walk down the aisle, Angie and Mary turned to check out their reflections in the glass doors and saw wings. They looked at each other in surprise and looked back—the wings were gone. They were beaming. They knew what they had seen.

The "Wedding March" started. Smiles spread over their grooms' faces as the brides linking arms with their dad glided down the aisle. Lost in their happiness, they hardly heard what was being said, but when it came time for the priest to bless them, they saw Jesus bless them too with Mary by his side. Angie glanced at Mary—they both knew the other had seen that as well.

When they were pronounced husbands and wives, the grooms were instructed to kiss their brides. The clapping that erupted brought them back to reality. They practically skipped down the aisle while "Good Vibrations" by the Beach Boys accompanied them.

After a long greeting line, they walked outside and were bombarded by bubbles. Yes, bubbles. No one wasted rice or bird seed. The bubbles glistened as they reflected the colors of double rainbows. Angie smiled and gave a thank-you to her rainbow archangel, Raziel. She swore she saw him smile back.

As their guests entered the reception hall, the newlyweds and their parents took photos on a footbridge that spanned a babbling brook. Ariel had found the place; it resembled the meet-and-greet area. They were happy in love.

It was time for them to make their grand entrance. When they saw musical notes out of the corners of their eyes, they knew Sandalphon was there and had selected love songs for them to dance the night away. "Top of the World" by the Carpenters was playing as their guests stood and clapped. The newlyweds took their seats. Stunning centerpieces of white and pink roses highlighted the white linen tablecloths and pink cloth napkins. Toasting glasses were filled and at the ready.

Archangel Sandalphon's music selections were surpassing their wildest dreams. He had appropriately selected "Something" by George Harrison for their first dance. As their guests sang along, they changed the pronouns from "she" to "they." Twirling around the dance floor, they danced with each other and their parents, families, and friends. The newlyweds saw the archangels twirling among them with their favorite colors accenting the dance floor. Their guests thought it was special lighting, but Angie knew the archangels were singing, dancing, tapping their toes, and enjoying themselves. She knew they were celebrating love. Chamuel had worked on the reception seating plans to ensure that all guests loved those they were seated next to. The love in the air was contagious. Everyone was having a wonderful time.

Their new friends and Loving Vibrations associates were there to rejoice in their celebrations as well. Angie was delighted that they had brought their loved ones. They had all been working so hard together, and seeing them relaxing and enjoying themselves was gratifying.

Ariel's expertise also included the menu selections of healthy, delectable vegan dishes, and all the meat lovers there had no idea. While they ate, a hush had come over the room. The only sounds were silverware meeting china—a very good sign of a delicious meal being enjoyed by all. Occasionally, someone would tap a goblet with a spoon or fork, and that prompted a delightful twinkling chorus that continued until kisses were exchanged by the brides and their grooms.

Their wedding cake was a masterpiece. Chocolate and vanilla layers were covered in a scrumptious vanilla-cream frosting. Roses in pink, green, and blue surrounded the many tiers of the cake, and two bride-and-groom cake toppers were perched above. Angie squeezed Mary's hand as she sent up her silent thank-you to Ariel. Everything was perfect.

Their guys removed the garters, and Matthew laughed when they saw Mary was wearing a pink one. Garters were tossed followed by the tossing of the bouquets. Dancing and merriment continued as the newlyweds changed into travel clothes. They were showered with more bubbles as they ran to the waiting limo that would take them to the airport. Manny, Cosmo, and Casey followed. They all flew to the conference continuing their merriment on the plane in which other passengers gleefully joined.

Their Hawaiian Loving Vibrations conference was a smashing success. Love was in the air as their attendees departed to spread love far and wide. The foursome bid their friends and associates goodbye as they stayed to enjoy their honeymoon.

There was a full moon their first night, and Angie thanked Haniel for keeping the clouds away. As they sat on the beach holding hands under the moonlit sky, they reminisced about Loving Vibrations, their spectacular wedding and enjoyable honeymoon, and their hopes and dreams for their new home together.

After several days of relaxation and enjoying each other, it was time to head back to reality. As soon as they returned, they had an appointment to see the home Metatron had told them about. Until then, Angie and Andrew would stay with the girls' parents and Mary and Matthew would stay with the guys' parents.

CHAPTER 36

Home Sweet Home Featuring Archangels Metatron and Ariel

When their realtor drove them up the driveway, they were amazed to find a mansion with gardens everywhere. The gardens were a wonderful sight. They saw every kind of flower imaginable and many they had never seen before. A paintbrush from heaven had left a riot of color all around the house.

Angie remarked to the others, "The fairies will love living here among the gardens. Ariel surely was the behind all this beauty. Look at that porch. It wraps around the home. We'll sit and enjoy the fairies at night."

Mary chimed in. "And look at that front door! Can you imagine a big Christmas wreath of fragrant pine needles and pine cones with some red ribbons?"

They nodded at that. They stepped through the front door and saw a magnificent staircase. Mary continued with her Christmas thoughts. "We can wrap garland up and down the handrails and include some bright-red bows. The fireplace will be a perfect place to hang our Christmas stockings. And can't you just see a giant Christmas tree decorated with angels and twinkling lights that will shine outside and shower the front porch with glistening light for the fairies?"

They toured the downstairs with visions of Christmas in their minds. After checking out the grand living room, they checked out the den. With Angie's love of books, she excitedly pointed out, "Look at the shelves of hardbound books reaching from the floor to the ceiling! They've rented a furnished home for us. Does that include the books?"

They were told everything would remain as they saw it. Angie was ready to sign on the dotted line even before she saw the kitchen or bedrooms.

Mary had run ahead to the kitchen and called out, "Angie, come and see. The appliances are all new. The counter top is granite, and look how it blends with the wooden cabinets. Can't you just see us sharing meals around the beautiful dining room table? It's big enough for our parents to join us. What should our first meal be? We should plan a celebration menu for our housewarming."

Angie found herself speechless as she was daydreaming about what Mary was saying. The guys had gone upstairs taking more of an interest in where they would be sleeping as opposed to matters of cooking. The guys called out, "Angie and Mary, come up here quickly. You have to see this!"

Andrew became their tour guide. "Look at the top of these stairs. There's a bedroom on the left with a sitting room, and another bedroom on the right with a sitting room. We can each have our own side. They each have their own bathrooms too. And there's another bathroom downstairs. Try out the beds. They're so comfortable!"

They ran to try out their beds. Matthew agreed with Andrew. "These beds are comfortable. I could fall asleep right now with Mary in my arms."

Laughter rang out. They hurried back downstairs as they agreed that everything about the home answered all their wishes and dreams. They liked having separate areas in case they wanted to be alone but close enough to pop over to spend time together.

Angie broke their spell. "How can we afford this place? It's huge, and our business is still growing."

Archangel Metatron, who had been with them but out of sight, appeared and explained, "I have a secret I'll share. This house has a reputation for being haunted."

As the fantasy bubble seemed to pop, Metatron quickly added, "Don't worry. I've taken care of that already. A couple of souls didn't want to cross over because they loved their home so much. They chased away everyone who tried to live here. Azrael met with the ghosts and assured them they would find their cherished home in heaven and it would be better there because they would have friends and family they would socialize with on the other side. They would have grand parties like they used to have. They were very enthusiastic to join Azrael, so off they went."

Metatron continued as he heard their collective sigh of relief. "The realtor and the home owner won't know that the home is ghost-free. They have tried to sell or rent the house for years and have had to return deposits time and again after the ghosts made it impossible for anyone to live there. Despite the furnishings, upgrades, new appliances, and all the comforts that were added to the home, nothing worked. Therefore, the rent on this place is extremely affordable. The homeowner kept hoping to find someone the ghosts would let stay there. The homeowner will believe that the ghosts like you. In time, he will be happy to sell the house to you. Everyone will be a winner in the end."

They returned to the realtor and signed the rental contract; the house was theirs. Angie's and Mary's birthdays were almost there, and Christmas was just a couple of weeks later. They were excited to celebrate Christmas as married couples in their own home. The guys moved them in while the girls put up Christmas decorations. Loving Vibrations was growing, so they were anxious to get this part of their earthly journey settled quickly.

Ariel had met with the fairies to explain that Angie and Mary were moving to a big new home and that the fairies needed to relocate. Ariel gave them directions. That night, Ariel returned to help them move. They absolutely loved their new home and were anxious to select their favorite plants or leaves to curl up in. They could take shelter from the rain in a woodshed there. They were assured that they would shift to the new Earth soon and would find this same house decked out in all its finery.

CHAPTER 37

The Meeting Featuring All Archangels

One night, Angie, Mary, Andrew, and Matthew were summoned to a special meeting with the archangels, guardian angels, and Legna. The meeting had a tone to it much more serious than their other educational and enjoyable visits. Everyone gathered in a private area in the Tapestry Room. After greetings and archangel hugs, they got down to business.

Archangel Michael spoke first. "Congratulations on your marriages, your new home, and especially Loving Vibrations. Everything is moving forward according to plan. Thank you, Metatron, for your research and coordination, and we thank all the archangels. However, our timetable has been shortened. The situation on the earthly plane is dire. Hateful people have been clouding the free-will choices of many loving souls and turning them dark. Some may not be saved. The shift must happen much sooner than anticipated. Preparations are in full swing. We need to make every effort to raise the vibrations of the remaining loving souls.

"Please understand that you have already done an extraordinary job. Billions of loving souls have raised their vibrations, and they have helped their family and friends raise their vibrations too. Let's work quickly to save the rest."

Archangel Metatron said, "Work extra hard to encourage enrollment in your internet school. Offer extraordinary discounts. Hold contests with multiple winners of free enrollment prizes. Ariel will make sure your expenses are covered. Increase the number of Loving Vibration conferences. Angie and Andrew will work together on multiple conferences while Mary and Matthew work on others thus doubling your efforts.

"I will assist you in coordinating the worldwide tours that will have you leading conferences in areas where vibrations remain at the lower levels. You will continue to be guest speakers at conferences held by others. Manny, Cosmo, and Casey will split up and attend many conferences individually. When they cannot attend in person, you can use their videos."

"How can we be sure that only the good souls attend and shift?" Angie asked. "I understand we will recognize the good souls, but what can we do with the negative souls?"

"Your jobs are to raise the vibrations," Metatron said, "not to worry about the actual shift. When every loving soul has reached the higher vibration, we will be ready. It will be the job of the Creator with his band of archangels to instantly shift all the souls to the new planet Earth. Negative souls will not shift."

"What about us?" asked Angie. "Will we shift with all the loving souls?"

"Absolutely," Archangel Michael responded. "After a celebration, you will find yourself on the new planet Earth. Your home will shift with you as will all the homes and neighborhoods of the loving souls. Don't worry—the fairies and all the elementals will shift along with you and all the other loving souls. Remembrances of the negative souls will be wiped from the memories of all the loving souls. Let us not have any further talk of celebrations until we complete our mission."

Angie had more questions, but she was assured there was no such thing as an unwelcomed question. "Legna, what about all the different groups of ETs? Don't some of them live underground or under the water on Earth?"

Legna was pleased with her concern. "We appreciate that you are worried about us, but don't be. My job is to make sure all the extraterrestrials relocate to the new Earth. Their vibrations were already raised many lifetimes ago. They do not need to shift. They can travel there by thought. Their job of trying to save the old Earth is over. Now, we will stand by in the event we must disarm a weapon or bring about a natural disaster to stall the inevitable.

"Most of the ETs have already been sharing their vast knowledge on the new planet. They had not been able to share their knowledge before because of the greedy and power-hungry people who were in charge on the old Earth. Those negative souls would've abused advanced technology for their own gain. That has happened time and again. Nuclear technology was turned into weapons of mass destruction. When the shift is complete, I promise you will meet many tribes of ETs. They will explain where they hail from and their specialties."

Angie responded, "Thank you, Legna. This is something we will look forward to. I'm pleased to learn they are all taken care of in their relocation to the new planet Earth."

Legna nodded. "If there are no other questions or concerns, I must leave. There is still much work to be done."

Angie had another question that had been bothering her. "Archangel Michael, can you explain to us about the souls who are born male or female but had tendencies toward the opposite gender? I'm not being judgmental. Are there good souls among them?"

Michael said, "Angie, do not think in terms of groups of people being good or bad. Souls do not have a gender. All souls have incarnated as both male and female throughout time. It is part of the necessary schooling to live as both male and female. When souls make plans for incarnation, they decide which gender would best help them enrich their soul. After they pass through the veil of forgetfulness, they're born the gender they had selected. Some carry too many soul memories from their past incarnation and don't remember they had decided to switch genders in this lifetime. Their life purpose remains the same regardless of their gender.

"On the other hand, some souls want to incarnate as cross gender to enrich their souls and those of others who will come into their lives. Only the souls can judge themselves. Love is the answer, not someone's life choice. You have the gift of recognizing the vibrations of loving souls, and that is all you will need. Now I must say goodbye and good luck. Thank you for your dedication to this mission. May you go in love and peace."

Michael bid them farewell for the time being and told them he would appear to them when the time was right to start working on the shift. In the meantime, he would remain close by.

Angie directed her next question to Archangel Ariel. "What about everyone's pets? When souls shift, will their beloved pets shift with them?"

Archangel Ariel said, "The bond between loving humans and their pets is unbreakable. Therefore, when humans shift, their pets will automatically shift."

Angie was relieved. The thought of pets being left behind without care was unthinkable.

Ariel continued. "As far as wild animals are concerned, I'll make sure they do not shift. On the new Earth, all the animals will be plant eaters. Unfortunately, many of the wild beasts have the inherent desire to eat meat. Those will not shift. We have the DNA of all animals from the beginning of time when no animals were killers. The new Earth will have all the same species as the old Earth with one big difference—the animals of the new Earth will be gentle and loving and will never harm a human being or any animal or fish. Imagine gently roughing up the mane of a lion as it sits before you nestling with a gentle lamb. It will happen. Sharks and all other sea dwellers will feast on seaweed and grasses, and there will be plenty for all.

"You will be happy to know that you will find all the extinct creatures on the new Earth. No one will hunt animals for their tusks or horns. The gentle and mystical creatures, the unicorns, will romp freely. The new Earth is already populated with animals of all types. The ocean and lakes are teeming with marine life. Birds, butterflies, and all other winged creatures are already enjoying peace in their new home."

Angie remarked, "Andrew and I saw the unicorns on the heavenly plane. They are magnificent creatures. I can't want to get to know them better. It will be awesome for everyone to enjoy them on the new Earth. But why don't our pets live as long as we humans do?"

Ariel explained, "That's another very good question that has several parts to it. Pets can move to a higher vibrational level and incarnate into human form because humans have individualized them with their love. To keep the movement going forward, all animals have been given shorter life spans to give them more opportunities to move up the vibrational levels.

"Also, Earth is a school in which humans must learn grief and bereavement. The loss of their pets helps them prepare for the loss of their beloved ones. That will change slightly. Like the ETs, the human souls will live much longer on the new Earth because there will be no disease or danger.

"When pets are ready to incarnate into human form, they will not die. We will know they are ready, and we will help them make that change. Your pet Dalmatian, Wendy, was with you during your recent childhood. She is ready to incarnate to the new Earth and will be part of your human family. You showered her with so much love and treated her with respect; that gave her the tools to raise her vibrational level."

Angie smiled at Andrew, Mary, and Matthew, who returned her smile as she said, "Wendy was so human. She understood a large vocabulary, loved people, and even attempted to talk. She will make a great loving human. I can't wait to have her as part of our family on the new Earth. But is there any way to stop the destruction and save the old planet Earth before the shift starts?"

Michael returned to explain, "In years past, there might have been a chance, but no longer. The Earth is too far gone and can no longer be saved."

"What about the Bible? Revelations?" Angie asked. "Don't we have to follow what was written?"

"You don't have to worry about revelations or any Bible passages, prophecies, or predictions," Michael said. "They were written a very long time ago as a warning to humankind. It gave humans an idea of what could happen. There was always hope that those warnings would encourage people to keep love in their hearts for all God's creatures. If they had, the new planet Earth and the shift would not have been necessary.

"Do not concern yourselves with the state of anyone's soul. Your mission is to raise the vibrations of the loving souls. The angels have been nudging all souls to make good, loving choices. Those who have turned dark will sit in judgment of themselves. You are to continue to practice love by setting a good example. Remember that you cannot teach people anything until they are ready to be taught. You cannot teach a preschooler algebra, and the same is true of the souls on Earth. You cannot teach them love if their hearts are closed. Love is the simple universal language that many still don't understand. Do your best, my dear children. Please raise the vibrations of the remaining loving souls as quickly as you can. When we are ready, you will experience two miracles signaling the beginning of the shift. I look forward to seeing you then."

Michael departed the group with loving thoughts for everyone. They agreed they were all ready and would anxiously await their miracles signaling that the shift was ready to begin.

Metatron concluded the meeting. "I have figured out your travel plans allowing you to attend conferences in cities spanning the globe. You will attend two to three conferences per day whenever possible. When you book your tickets, you will always find there are four tickets available. Ground transportation will be simple to arrange. At each of the conferences, throngs of loving souls will be nudged to raise their vibrations. They will take this knowledge and tell their friends, who will tell their friends, and so on. The tide of loving vibrations will continue to spread over the Earth."

"My mom used to say, 'Don't look at the mountain. Instead, chip away at the mountain,'" Angie said. "That got me through many a daunting task. She also used to say not to think about the dreaded situation you are currently experiencing such as being at the dentist's office. Instead, think ahead to being home and the fun you'll have later. We must apply that here. We won't think about how many conferences or the millions of loving souls. We will keep chipping away at the mountain while we look forward to our next banquet in the meet-and-greet area."

Archangel Michael responded, "Exactly, my dear one." The others nodded. "It is now time for you to return to your beds. In the morning, pack your bags and make your reservations. Metatron will imprint the schedule in your minds before you leave. Don't hesitate. Once this starts, it must be completed quickly. We will meet back here to discuss your progress."

CHAPTER 38

The Miracles and a Kiss from Above
Featuring Archangel Michael

Angie and Mary had enjoyed their birthday celebrations in their new home. It was time to celebrate Christmas. They made sure their house looked like a fairyland with twinkling lights everywhere as they had planned. A huge Christmas wreath adorned their front door. Their banisters were encircled with garland and red ribbons. Their stockings hung by the fireplace in the shadow of a dazzling tree decked out with angel ornaments.

They planned a delicious feast that would leave them with plenty of leftovers. The girls cooked while the guys helped. Their help consisted of much sampling "to ensure that the dishes passed the taste test," they said. They had no complaints.

Soon, both sets of parents had arrived in the same car as part of the plan for the event that was to unfold later that evening. They pushed those thoughts out of the way. The Christmas lights shined out into the night casting a magical paradise for the fairies. Christmas carols filled their home along with the fragrance of pine that wafted from their scented candles. The kitchen smelled of cinnamon, herbs, and butter. They toasted in the holiday and nibbled on appetizers as the twins opened their special keepsake gifts. The parents had put together photo albums and a photomontage on CDs commemorating their childhoods.

Angie thanked them. "This is the perfect gift. We will treasure these memories!"

The others nodded as they held back tears of joy mingled with sadness at the thought of what was to come. They enjoyed a delicious meal followed by scrumptious desserts of chocolate cake, cookies, brownies, and even some angel food cake with fresh strawberries. They didn't want the night to end.

It had been determined that all their parents had completed their lives' purposes on the earthly plane and could better assist from the heavenly plane. The eight of them had met with the archangels and guardian angels and decided that the parents would be in a terrible car accident on their way home from their Christmas celebration. They would all die instantly, and Azrael would be there to help them cross over.

It would seem tragic to everyone except the foursome and their parents. They would have their second Christmas celebration during their meet-and-greet party that night. Angie, Andrew, Mary, and Matthew would attend during their dream time.

The twins hugged their parents very tightly and waved as they drove away. They settled down to wait for the police to arrive at their door with the horrific news. Angie said, "We need to act mortified and shed real tears. Push away thoughts about the merriment that awaits us later tonight." Everyone agreed with that.

The police arrived with the tragic news. The twins acted their parts and even requested an investigation into the crash. They bid the police goodbye with tear-filled eyes.

As they shut the door, Andrew reminded them, "Let's hurry and get settled in our beds. The sooner we fall asleep, the sooner we can enter dream time and join the celebration on the astral plane. Angie and Mary, come on! You can clean up the kitchen in the morning. We'll help you then. Time's a' wasting."

Angie and Mary agreed with Andrew; they left the kitchen and were soon snuggled in their beds where their husbands were already drifting off to sleep. Before they realized it, they were in the gardens outside the meet-and-greet area on the astral plane. Their parents looked very happy and welcomed them with open arms. Their Dalmatians came bounding over. Angie heard her sons yell out, "Hi, Mom!" She had heard them say hi to her every time it was 12:11 when they looked at their clocks. She hugged them, and Andrew did too. Happiness and love filled the air. A full moon had chased away the setting sun. It was time for the banquet.

Their parents took seats at the head of the table. Angie and Andrew sat on one side while Mary and Matthew sat on the other. Their sons joined them. The seats filled up with family and friends. Delicious food was served by angels flitting around personally attending to everyone's desires. Stories were shared, and laughter rang out. It was a glorious second Christmas celebration, a night they would always cherish.

Before they said their goodbyes, Angie, Andrew, Mary, and Matthew went outside to admire the full moon leaving its diamond pathway on the babbling brook. They stood in silence admiring their surroundings. They saw the unicorns having their nightly drink.

Angie broke the spell. "This will probably be the last time we enjoy such a delightful celebration for a while. I'm confident the shift will start soon and we will be extremely busy. Let's take in the essence of this evening. Let's inhale some deep breaths of pure love and exhale any negatives in us. We have been through a lot tonight. Let's do some cord-cutting together."

Archangel Metatron appeared to help them clear their chakras. When they were done, Angie heard a resounding "Amen!" It was time to go. They woke up in their beds on Earth. It was time to plan the funeral arrangements for their parents that Azrael had helped organize. They wished they could explain to the mourners that their parents were happy and watching over them. They wanted to let everyone know there had been a heavenly party, but they knew they couldn't tell anyone. Who would believe them anyway?

They worked hard on Loving Vibrations and were very pleased with the number of loving souls who had taken the courses and attended the conferences. Despite the overpowering negativity that had spread throughout the planet, thousands upon thousands of loving souls encouraged them. They anxiously waited for their first sign.

It was September—hurricane season. A major hurricane was bearing down on the Caribbean islands with landfall expected to hit the southern tip of Florida as a category 5. They lived eighty miles north. The hurricane shutters were up, and all outdoor furniture had been brought in.

They created a special area in their den for the fairies full of all their outdoor and indoor potted plants. They invited them in and watched as they selected their favorite sleeping petals and leaves. There were so many of them, but they would all be safe; Ariel would make sure of that. They had no doubt that regardless of how scary the storm was that night, the fairies would still dance the night away.

Candles, batteries, water, and canned food were ready. There was nothing left to do but pray. The landfall prediction had the hurricane coming right up the middle of the state. The tremendous storm would cover Florida from east to west and south to north. Pictures of the devastation that the islands had suffered were sad and scary. They couldn't leave. Where could they go? The shelter was two blocks from their house. They would stay home. Their evacuation plan would be to walk to the shelter if their home became uninhabitable.

They held hands and prayed constantly reciting, "We love our home and family. If we haven't seemed appreciative, please believe us we are. Archangel Michael, please put a protective shield around us and our home and all the homes. Ariel, please take care of the fairies."

Around 5:00 p.m., darkness fell. They heard a thud but could not see what it was. They noticed through a window in their door that it was totally dark out front, but looking through the window in the back door let them know it was daylight out in that direction. The winds and rain were too ominous for them to venture outside to investigate. They checked the ceilings, and all appeared fine.

After a fitful night, Angie woke up first. "Let's go outside and see what happened. The winds have subsided, and it's getting light out. We must find out what that noise was and why it still looks so dark out our front door."

After confirming that the fairies were fine and settled in for their daytime sleep, they ventured out into the yard and gasped when they saw that their three-story sea grape tree had splintered like a matchstick. Many of its sturdy limbs had snapped. One heavy limb was leaning on their roof, but there didn't appear to be any damage except maybe a bent gutter. The limb must have slowly cracked and gently lay down on their roof. It was a miracle. They did some minor cleanup and headed indoors thanking the Lord and Archangel Michael.

As Angie looked down at her phone, she gasped, "Look! Archangel Michael is on my phone with the caption 'Divine Light!' How did that get there? This must be a sign that Archangel Michael has been with us."

As they entered their home, Angie gasped again. "Look! It's eleven twenty-seven—Mom's birthday. I know our parents watched over us through this storm."

Andrew and Angie checked out the news on TV and read the day's messages from their angel calendar. Then they pulled an oracle card. Both were part of their morning ritual. The card they pulled was from Archangel Michael and was entitled, "You Are Safe." The caption read, "I am protecting you against lower energies and guarding you, your loved ones, and home."

Angie called over to Mary and Matthew, "Come here quick! You must see this! This must be another sign from Archangel Michael! He watched over us. That huge tree limb fell so gently that it didn't do any damage! We're safe, and we hardly had any rainfall! We were spared!"

Prayers of gratitude rang out. They had had their first miracle. Their second miracle wasn't far behind, and it also involved bad weather.

A huge storm was approaching. The alert warnings signaled them that there was lightning in their area. It was 2:00 a.m., and a check of the weather radar on Angie's mobile phone showed an intense storm approaching their home. She called to the others, "Wake up! We have another storm coming, and it's bad. We must get the fairies in."

They called out to Archangel Ariel for help as they ran outside yelling to the fairies, "Come quickly! You all must come inside! There's a very bad storm coming! Stop your dancing, and call out to everyone to come in! You can stay in our living room downstairs. We will leave some soft light on, and you can dance and continue your partying in safety."

Masses of fairies flew up the porch and into their living room while Mary held the door open. The fairies hardly noticed as their rescuers bid them goodnight; they continued dancing without missing a beat.

Before they parted for their own beds, Angie told them about the weather prediction for the night. They were expected to get three to four hours of intense rain with the possibility of tornadoes, lightning, and of course thunder. As she spoke, thunder cracked right over their heads. They dashed to their beds hugging each other tightly.

From her bed, Angie led them in prayer, "Dear Creator, archangels, and our guardian angels, please keep us safe on this awful night. Archangel Michael, please put a protective shield around our house. Archangel Ariel, please protect the fairies. We thank you, amen."

They waited in silence. It wasn't long before Angie could tell that Andrew was sleeping. She was restless and put on her favorite angel meditation tape. As she relaxed and cleared her negative, fearful energies, she was instructed to replace the negative feelings with positive energies. Suddenly, Angie felt a kiss. She was startled. She slowly opened her eyes expecting to see Andrew, but it was not him. She saw Michael kissing her forehead. At first, she thought she was dreaming until she heard him say, "It is time. Go in peace to save the loving souls." The storm stopped. Everything was quiet. Their prayers had been answered. Thinking she might have been dreaming, she fell into a deep sleep.

She opened her eyes to sunlight. It was morning. There were no puddles or flooding or any evidence of rain. The picture from their morning internet newspaper clearly showed they we were in the center of a huge storm. Regardless of what the newspaper or numerous weather radar maps had shown, they had experienced nothing. Instead, they received a miracle, an answered prayer, a blessing, a kiss. Extreme calm settled over Angie all day. *How wonderful!* And then she recalled Michael's words.

They peeked in the living room and saw that the fairies were settled in for their daytime sleep. They agreed to leave them there until nightfall when they could return to the outdoors and party the night away.

Angie explained to the others what had happened the night before. She repeated Michael's exact words, "It is time. The vibrations have all been raised. Go in peace to dwell with the loving souls." They all agreed that they had received the second sign and that it was time for the shift to begin.

Angie was ready, but she wanted to know the exact details of how the shift would happen. "We have conferences scheduled for Europe including plans to visit the Vatican. I wonder if that is where it will start. If loving souls are to shift from outside the Vatican, there should be surveillance cameras."

Mary responded, "Don't worry, Angie. I'm sure those in charge will handle everything. Let's wait for additional guidance from above."

CHAPTER 39

The Shift Featuring Archangels Michael and Chamuel

They were summoned to a special meeting during their dream time that night. Archangel Michael introduced them to Archangel Chamuel, whom they had only briefly met before. He was beautiful and stoic yet peaceful. His aura was a pale green like the early morning sunlight peeking through spring leaves and glistening in the dew.

"It's a pleasure to officially meet all of you," Chamuel said. "From the beginning, I've been observing and assisting you from behind the scenes. You are to be commended for raising the vibrations of billions of loving souls."

Archangel Michael continued with the introduction. "Archangel Chamuel's name means he who sees God. He sees the connection between the Creator and everyone and everything. His very important task is achieving universal peace. The Creator put him in charge of the physical shift after all vibrations have been raised. You raised the vibrations, and we are ready."

Archangel Chamuel continued. "Angie, as you have asked before and understanding your loving soul, I'd like to explain my feelings, which are very similar to yours. My quest for universal peace makes it very difficult for me to leave any negative souls behind. I look for the good in all souls, but I realize the old Earth is dying and only the good, loving souls will shift to the new Earth.

"The negative souls will perish and leave their earthly bodies. Their souls will be saved by resting and attending school on the astral plane. They'll have their chance at salvation when they incarnate to another primitive planet. Those who had been living in huge buildings will be grateful to find a cave to live in. Those who have had the bounties of life deposited at their feet will find themselves toiling for every scrap of food. It is befitting that those who have caused so much damage will have to start over again on the lowest rung on the human ladder of life. There is no sense dwelling on the negative souls. It's time. I will escort you to the Creator so you can all witness the shift before you join the loving souls on the new planet Earth."

Jesus and Mary met them, and they all ascended as Angie had done before. She loved seeing the reactions of Andrew, Mary, and Matthew, who were silenced by the awe of their surroundings.

They were holding hands as Angie communicated to them through their thoughts. "We are in the presence of the Creator. Those are the archangels gliding around the room in their Aurora Borealis display of their auras. You can recognize them by their colors. The billions of lights surrounding the outer walls are all the souls. The vast majority are shining brightly revealing their higher vibrations."

Chamuel stopped swirling in his leafy greenery to stand next to the brilliant light of the Creator. At that moment, the stars on the outer wall changed. There were hardly any stars visible. Chamuel let them know they were looking at the old planet Earth.

Chamuel proclaimed as the dark instantly became a sparkling mosaic of the brightest lights, "It is done. You are now looking at the new planet Earth. The shift is complete."

Jesus added, "And so it is done. Thank you, Angie, Andrew, Mary, and Matthew for your assistance in raising the vibrations and making the shift possible. We could not have done it without you. Thank you to our band of angels and archangels, to Legna and all the ETs, and to Casey, Manny, and Cosmo. This was a very successful team effort. Tonight, Angie, Andrew, Mary, and Matthew will wake up in their favorite house and in their comfy beds on the new Earth never to return to the old Earth again."

Angie asked, "When will the old Earth disappear so only the new Earth will remain?"

Archangel Michael explained it. "In the time it takes for the full moon to appear, in about a month based on Earth time, the planets will shift. The old Earth will implode and vanish as the new Earth will slide into its place. During that month, all hell will break loose on the old Earth. There will be every disaster known to humanity—earthquakes, volcanos, and melting polar ice caps. Farmland will dry up in a severe drought. The waters will be polluted and undrinkable. Insects will be everywhere spreading fatal diseases. The surviving negative souls will need to face what they have wrought upon the Earth. That is the only way they will understand.

"During their life reviews, they will see what they have done. When they make plans to work out their karma for their next incarnation, they will face challenges they have not had to face since primitive times. Right before the old planet Earth implodes, all negative souls will shift to the heavenly plane, where they will go through the light and immediately to the resting area. They will remain there for a long period until their souls are cleared. Then, they'll have a long period of adjustment before they are incarnated to one of the primitive planets in the far reaches of the solar system to start life anew. The Bible warns that you will reap what you sow. They had been warned, and now, it is so.

"You have raised the vibrations of billions, and we are raising your vibrations even higher. With every increase, you will became closer to the Creator's vibrational level and have an increased knowledge of the universe. As you know, you are not required to dwell on the earthly plane, but we strongly suggest that you remain there for now and for as long as you want. It will be good for all of you to enjoy the loving planet you were instrumental in bringing to fruition. While on the earthly plane, you will continue to have clear seeing, clear hearing, clear feeling, clear knowing, and the ability to see the good vibrations of loving souls. But it's now time for a celebration. The angels will join you in the meet-and-great area tonight. Your family and friends are waiting. Go and enjoy."

No sooner had the words been spoken than they found themselves there with their parents and Angie's and Andrew's sons. They had witnessed everything as they watched from their observation post in the heavens. They embraced and thanked each other. It was time for a victory celebration with their departed family, friends, and many they did not know—loving souls that had passed just before the shift. The angels and archangels had joined them too. It was a joyous evening.

The next morning, they would wake up in their beds on the new Earth to work with all the loving souls. They would return during dream times for future guidance and instructions, but for the time being, their mission was accomplished. They would enjoy an Earth where there was no violence. Imagine all the people living in harmony and getting along with no government, no religion, no rules to break, and no humans or animals to fear. They were anxious to start enjoying this new Earth.

CHAPTER 40

Mission Accomplished—
Peace on the New Earth

After their reunion and victory celebration, they woke up in their beds. There was no rush to wake up; they enjoyed each other before going downstairs. The girls made breakfast. They ate and planned their day.

Angie suddenly bolted from the table and ran out the front door. The others followed in hot pursuit wondering what the matter was. Angie stood on the porch smiling. She saw the fairies settled into their petals for their daytime sleep. She thought about the looking glass they had originally needed to see them. She looked toward the others, and they saw them too. Angie ran back inside to get the looking glass, and when she returned, she hung it on the porch column to remind them of the time on the old Earth when it was needed.

They cleaned up the kitchen and got ready to spend a delightful day exploring. They decided not to make any specific plans but to let the day take them where it may. Before they stepped off the porch to start their adventure that day, they held hands and offered up a prayer of thanks to their Creator and all their archangels and guardian angels.

The Creator could have let the planet implode with everyone on it including all the loving souls and make them all start over again, but he hadn't. He gave the loving souls a chance to live in a paradise, and they were to enjoy every minute of it. They all vowed never to forget their past and to always call on their archangels and guardian angels when in need. They would make that a daily ritual. As they stepped off their porch every morning, they would stop, hold hands, and offer up a prayer of thanks.

They skipped to town that day past beautiful fields. They saw unicorns romping through the flowers but never hurting a single petal. A huge lion with a gorgeous mane walked past them and rubbed against their legs just as a house cat would. It would take them time to get used to not being afraid. They saw a bear scratching his back against a tree. When he saw them, he came over and went down on all fours so they could scratch his back for him. Butterflies were everywhere. They knew they were a sign from heaven and sent up a hello to their parents and sons. They would see them soon as they were planning to incarnate to the new Earth.

Everyone they saw greeted them with smiles and happy thoughts. They did not have to speak. Everyone had the gift of telepathic communication and could read others' thoughts. They passed one house and saw a man carrying something that looked too heavy for him. The foursome heard his thoughts and joined him to complete the task. He didn't have to speak a thank-you because his thoughts conveyed how appreciative he was.

The birds filled the air with melodious song. Sandalphon must have had his influence in filling the new Earth with music. They saw multiple rainbows. Angie was glad that Archangel Raziel continued to send his rainbow signs reminding everyone to take a moment to thank the Creator for the beauty signified by a rainbow. Since there would no longer be daytime rains, Angie had worried that rainbows would become part of the lost world. She should have realized that Raziel did not need raindrops to create rainbows.

They skipped to the town square. A calming, flute-like music filled their air. The gazebo came into view. Even in daylight, it was adorned in twinkling lights. People were milling everywhere. Children held hands in a circle moving in and out and raising their hands above their heads. Other children were playing kickball. Some adults were playing softball in a field while others were knitting and crocheting in a circle. They may never need the warmth of their creations, but that didn't matter. They were having fun, and it might get chilly on some nights.

A couple of restaurants offered all the selections one could possibly desire. They were all vegan in keeping with the plan that no animal would be killed for food. Food was not a requirement anyway; they would receive all their nutrients from the water, which was delicious. But it was fun to consume some favorite dishes and snacks too.

In the distance, they saw a magnificent flying saucer at the airport. It was exactly as they would have expected to see one—all shiny and saucer shaped, but it was massive. People had gone down to look. No one was guarding it or turning people away. There were no weapons. There was no need to be concerned because all people had only love in their hearts. Many different ETs were milling about; the smiles on everyone's face meant they could communicate telepathically.

Angie said that during dream time that night, she would ask Legna to meet with them so they could make plans to be introduced to the other ETs as had been promised. The others agreed.

All people had to get used to the changes; they had to learn to not be afraid of the gentle beasts. They didn't need umbrellas or raincoats when they went out in the daytime because it rained only at night and only enough to fill their reservoirs. They did not have to worry about natural disasters such as earthquakes, hurricanes, tornados, blizzards, and droughts. Those who wanted to live in a cold climate or participate in winter sports could do so at the higher elevations. For the most part, it would be springtime throughout the planet.

There would be no need for prisons because there would be no criminals. There would be no police, courts, lawyers, or juries, so there would be no jury duty. Those were all negative energies that had no place on the new planet. There was no need for hospitals or doctors. Germs and disease were also negative energies that could not survive in this loving environment. No one would get old either. Once they reached maturity, adults would retain their youthful looks and bodies throughout eternity.

There were no longer different countries throughout the world, so there was no need for borders and certainly no need for walls. All were free to go wherever they liked and would be welcomed everywhere. They all communicated telepathically. They had mouths and ears but mostly for music and singing. They had one universal language to communicate if they so choose. The spoken words were used primarily for songs and poetry.

As they returned their focus to the town square, a young girl approached them. She said that her name was Wendy and that she didn't have any parents there but needed a home. She had been guided to meet Angie and Andrew. Without hesitation, Angie threw her arms around Wendy, and Andrew made it a group hug. "We know and love you. Do you remember us?"

Wendy responded that she knew the minute they hugged her. Mary and Matthew ran over to join the hug. Wendy had been Mary's dog too, and Matthew had spent many an afternoon playing ball with her. They joined hands and headed toward their home, which was Wendy's home too.

CHAPTER 41

Homeward Bound Featuring Archangel Azrael

After about a month of thoroughly enjoying their new planet, no matter where they were, everyone felt the planet shudder. It was momentary, and it did no damage. It had happened. The old Earth was no more. The new planet had slid into place and would be the only planet Earth from that day forward. The far-reaching galaxies need no longer fear. If the old planet Earth had imploded without a replacement Earth, that would have sent shock waves throughout the universe. Planets would have been bumped out of their orbits with many colliding. The chain reaction would have destroyed everything everywhere except in the heavens. The Creator would have had to start over again and create the solar systems and habitable planets. The task would have been monumental and such a shame because of the greed and selfishness that had taken over the tiny inhabited planet called Earth. The four were sad that it had come to that but happy that it was over.

The next day, the foursome was transported to a huge UFO that was like a city in the sky above the new planet Earth. It remained out of sight.

Legna greeted them. "Welcome Angie, Andrew, Mary, and Matthew. I want you to meet some of the ETs you will see on the new Earth. As I explained, you do not have to remember their names because you will recognize them through your mutual thoughts."

Hundreds of ETs entered and said, "Greetings!"

In amazement, Angie commented, "I had no idea there were so many different ETs. Wow, this is amazing! And to think we will remember all of you once we communicate with you!"

Legna said, "There is more. You know that we possess a vast amount of knowledge. As we communicate with you, our knowledge will be imprinted on your souls."

Angie asked, "Will your knowledge be imprinted on everyone's soul?"

"Not necessarily," Legna said. "You were taught that you can't teach a kindergartener algebra. The same is true with our knowledge. Based on your increased vibration, we know the four of you are ready to receive all knowledge, but others will be receptive to only certain types of knowledge and will receive the knowledge they are ready to receive when they are ready for it."

Angie had so many questions that spilled out all at once. "Will you return to your families on other planets? Will they come here to visit you and see the new Earth? How will you travel? How will they travel? Will we get to meet them? Will we get to visit your planets?"

Legna had been used to Angie's questions. "Angie dear, where do I begin? Some of our families are here and stay with us onboard our craft. We travel back and forth by thought. You will get to meet many of them, and yes, someday, you will visit our planets, but not yet. Your vibrational levels have not reached that point yet, but I strongly believe that day will come for all of you."

Archangel Michael entered the gathering. "Greetings to one and all! Legna previously explained that the angels can meet you onboard their craft, so here I am. We discussed some of the special differences between the old and new Earths. Now that you are here, you will start to experience them, and a refresher discussion would be helpful. You experienced collective consciousness when you helped that man carry a heavy object."

"We did it without thinking about it, and it felt good!" Angie said.

"In time, you will learn to do things such as move heavy objects by thought without lifting a hand. That is how many of the pyramids megaton slabs slid into place. The ETs will review some of the topics we discussed before as I stand by."

Legna explained clean solar and wind energy. He introduced them to crystals with amazing properties. Some gave off light and were used in the houses and for streetlights. Some gave off an energy force like a conveyor belt. You could jump on the light beam and jump off when you reached your destination. Large items could be transported that way too; the ETs showed them how levitation worked. They joined hands and encircled an object. As they raised their hands, the object moved up. It took some practice, but they learned to move rocks and lumber into position. In no time, automobiles, trucks, machinery, and the like would become useless.

Archangel Michael completed the meeting by saying, "The ETs are always available and willing to share their knowledge with you. It is time to transport you back. You are welcome anytime."

The foursome wished them well. In an instant, they were back in their home.

The archangels visited them often, and the foursome frequently visited the heavenly plane and the ET craft. Everyone had at least two guardian angels who were always present. Everyone could communicate with them much more easily than they could on the old planet Earth.

Every once in a while, they were given the honor of visiting with Jesus and Mary and sometimes with the Creator. They had discussed how the Ten Commandments were no longer needed. The Commandments had been the guide to achieving a loving planet. Many of the Commandments dealt with offenses against humankind such as thou shalt not kill, steal, lie, cheat, and so on, but those negative behaviors no longer existed. It was a wonderful planet. The vision had been correct—the planet was full of loving souls living in peace and harmony.

Angie, Andrew, Mary, and Matthew thoroughly enjoyed the new planet Earth. Even with all the comforts surrounding them, they were never bored. They enjoyed getting outside and enjoying the company of other loving souls. Everyone had something to talk about. There were improvements to be made, and everyone pitched in and worked together. They did not need a natural disaster to encourage them to help their neighbors.

The fairies had scattered to bring joy to other families by taking up residence in gardens everywhere. Their special fairy, Sunshine, whom they had rescued from the tangled vines many years before, had remained with them. The entire original community of fairies they had met when they discovered the looking glass also stayed with them. Many a night was spent on their porch watching the fairies dance and sing. They no longer needed the warning system. Cats no longer bothered them. In fact, they saw cats twitching their tails in delight and in time to their music.

Wendy was a delight. They moved all the books from the den into the grand room and changed the den into Wendy's personal bedroom. When the others were upstairs in their bedrooms and sitting rooms, Wendy had the entire first floor to herself. When they visited the heavenly plane, Wendy would often come with them. She always attended parties at the meet-and-greet area. Wendy was especially fond of the fairies, and it was no surprise that she was an animal lover. She often volunteered to take care of pets while their owners were away.

She had many friends, and she was always bringing them over to her home. There was one guy, William, she really liked. They spent a lot of time together. It was no surprise when they announced they wanted to get married and start a family.

William was invited to move in with Wendy and share their home. They held a wedding ceremony in the gazebo in the town square. Everyone came and helped make their special day an event to remember. Some decorated the gazebo with fresh flowers. Others brought their favorite dishes. The children practiced singing the wedding march and danced around the gazebo. It was a very festive event.

That night during dream time, they all celebrated again in the meet-and-greet area with departed loved ones. Many of the archangels attended including Ariel, who had helped Wendy incarnate as a human. Jophiel had helped Wendy become a vision of loveliness for the occasions on Earth and in heaven. Frequently, earthly celebrations were also held on the heavenly plane so departed loved ones who had not incarnated yet could join the festivities.

Angie, Andrew, Mary, and Matthew lived a long life on the new planet Earth. They watched Wendy and William have their own children. It was no surprise when they had twins—a boy and a girl. They had become grandparents, great-grandparents, and even great-great-grandparents. They loved living in Paradise, but they longed to go home and enjoy the heavenly plane without the density of Earth. They longed to travel by thought. They all agreed the time had come.

They discussed their plans with Wendy and William, who totally understood. They were not sad because they could see them anytime they wanted during dream time. The foursome made a promise that if they ever incarnated again, they would incarnate together. After all, they were soul mates bound together for eternity.

That night when they traveled to the heavenly plane, they would not be returning. They kissed each other goodnight and lay on their beds on the earthly plane. Azrael was there to greet them. There was no need to leave signs for anyone they had left behind on the new Earth. All their friends could visit them during dream time. There would be many celebrations and parties in the meet-and-greet area.

Many things had changed. They did not need to go toward the light; they immediately found themselves surrounded by family and friends. After welcome-home greetings, they promised to return and went with Jophiel to freshen up. They would not be required to go through the resting stage. Soon, they were back with their loved ones. Their dogs came bounding over to greet them.

During their dream time, Wendy, William, and all their offspring joined them. All night, the food delighted their palates and stories filled the air. That time, the discussions focused on the wondrous new planet Earth and so many loving souls living in harmony. They were glad they would never again have to see or interact with the negative souls who had caused such destruction.

When the archangels had moved the negative souls through the different stages of clearing and wisdom, they kept them far away from the loving souls. When the time was right, they would incarnate on the primitive planet. They could not take the chance that any of their negative energy would befall the loving souls who filled the heavenly plane. Love had conquered all. Love was the answer. All they needed was love, love, love.

CHAPTER 42

The Next Mission

Angie, Andrew, Mary, and Matthew had spent time together enjoying life on the heavenly plane. One of their favorite pastimes was witnessing life on the new Earth. It was truly a paradise with loving souls everywhere working and playing together. They thoroughly enjoyed watching Wendy and William and all their offspring grow to adulthood. Everyone lived together in the big house. Wendy and William had kept their bedroom in the den so they could continue to enjoy the entire house when the others were upstairs. There were toys where Angie's favorite books used to be, but she didn't mind.

Sometimes, they wished they could visit their house filled with all their loved ones. They would have loved to take a vacation on the new Earth, but that was not possible without incarnating. They had learned to travel by thought and had been able to visit with the ETs on their planets throughout the galaxies, and that was great fun. There were so many loving and different ETs. No one on Earth could ever imagine how many planets in far-off galaxies were inhabited. Whomever they visited welcomed them with open arms and graciously spent time introducing them to their planets. On the heavenly plane, they could study more about the planets they visited. They considered those visits their vacations.

One night when they were summoned by Archangel Michael along with all the other archangels and their guardian angels, Michael said, "We've heard your wish to vacation on the new Earth. It will do you all well. We'd like you to incarnate there. You can call it a vacation if you like. You decide how long you wish to stay there.

When you are ready to return whether it be in a couple of weeks, months, or years, you will return.

"Your mission this time will be to live among the loving souls and use your talents and gifts to see if any souls are turning negative. You will be asked just to identify them, and we will take care of the rest. We do not suspect that there are any negative energies, but some souls might be showing signs of greed or a desire for power. We need to review and perhaps remove them.

"We'd like to send you as observers. You'll be granted one additional gift, and that is to teleport around the universe not only to this heavenly sphere but also to any of the planets in any of the galaxies. You'll not have to wait for dream time. And you'll be able to teleport to any of the spaceships that are beyond range from normal human eyesight. You'll see them and be able to visit them at will. These craft have the capability to view vast distances that you may find helpful. The choice is yours. Vacation is granted, but it is not mandatory. Will you take on this new task?"

To find out if Angie, Andrew, Mary, and Matthew will be saying, "Here we go again" or if they will retire and enjoy their lives on the heavenly plane, read the next book in the series, *Angel Blessings—Imagine*.

Afterword

I hope you have enjoyed taking this journey with Angie, Andrew, Mary, Matthew, and the archangels through the circle of life. It was a wonderful journey for me too following the daily guidance of Archangel Gabriel and never knowing quite where he would take me. Some mornings, I would wake up with an entire chapter in my mind. Other mornings, I would receive instructions to research a topic or even to attend a class.

I have learned to trust these messages. When I received my first message to write a book, I questioned it. When the message told me to research angels, I did so but still wondered what was going on. As the messages continued, it became evident that I was receiving divine guidance and that I should not question but instead do what I was being asked to do—let others know about their angels.

Our angels are all around us. We are never alone. We all have at least two guardian angels, and if we ask them for their names as we fall asleep, we might wake up with their names on our mind. I will never forget waking up to the message that one of my guardian angels gave me: "Arla, not Carla, but Arla." The voice in my mind was very clear and specific.

We should all ask for help no matter how small our requests are or how insignificant we think they are. We do not pray to angels; we pray to God or to the deity of our religion. Angels are included in all religions, but sometimes, they have different names. The word *angel* means "messenger of God." All souls, all angels, and even our Creator have different vibrational levels, the Creator being at the highest level. Sometimes, it's difficult for us to understand messages coming directly from the highest level. Angels bring the information to us because we can understand them. Another important detail to understand is that they are multidimensional; they can help many people at the same time.

We all have egos. The ego is the doubting Thomas that makes us doubt ourselves, so we should throw our doubts away. In the words of my loving mother, we can do anything we put our minds to. We all remember the story of the little engine that chugged up the hill saying, "I think I can I think I can" and then saying, "I know I can I know I can." We all can with the help of our angels and archangels.

Ask Archangel Michael to protect you and your family when traveling and to protect all those around you. Ask him to protect your house and all your possessions. Ask Archangel Raphael to help heal you. He may heal you or guide you to a doctor or a medicine that will help. And if you are in the field of communication, ask Archangel Gabriel to help you find the loving words to convey your message. Archangel Gabriel is also the archangel of children and is there to help. All the archangels have specific talents. If you don't know which archangel to call upon for help with your situation, reach out to them all.

Also, remember that our Creator is love. If you receive any negative or hurtful instructions, do not follow them. Do not be too specific in your requests. If you need money, don't ask to win the lottery. Your request might be answered in a different way that will be better for you.

Keep in mind that we have all made our life plans and mapped out our life purposes before we arrived on Earth. Certain plans cannot be changed, so if your request is not answered, perhaps it can't be. We may have chosen to live in poverty or to have an illness or suffer a disaster to learn a life lesson to enrich our souls. The bumps in the road of life may have been our choices before we got here.

Face each challenge with determination by asking your deity and the archangels and guardian angels for help and always with love in your heart. You have free will, so when you have a choice to make, always pick the loving path. If you have made mistakes in the past, don't fret. Every day is a new day and a chance to get on the path to a loving life.

Love is the answer to everything. Keep a smile on your face, and have compassion and understanding for all God's children.

Some may seem like idiots, but maybe they wanted to be that way for their souls to learn lessons and maybe teach others the lessons of patience, forgiveness, or acceptance. The way you treat people is imprinted on your soul. Learn your lessons well.

I hope to see you on Angie's next journey. Will Angie, Andrew, Mary, and Matthew return to the new Earth? Check www.pattycallahan.us for the next release date.

Do you have an angel story? Share your experience with the angel lovers throughout the world. Our third book, *Angel Blessings—Behold*, will feature your angel encounters. Submit your story through www.pattycallahan.us.

About the Author

Angel Blessings relays many of Patty's personal experiences. However, we are happy to report that Patty is alive and well. The incidents in chapter 3, "Signs Received," are true and are some of the many signs Patty has received over the years. If you look back on the twists and turns of your life, you may find signs too. There is no such thing as coincidence. It was necessary to have Angie pass over to be able to introduce you to the archangels.

Communication has always been Patty's forte, and her love of people has led to her many successes. She has always listened to the inner voice that wakes her up in the morning and guides her through her day. She rarely remembers her dreams. Instead, she wakes up to a gentle command. She thought it was her inner voice that had worked out situations in her dream state, but that theory changed when the voice told her to write a book. She let her imagination run wild, and she wrote many short stories that later became chapters in this book.

Her search for angels led her to the Hay House and its writing courses, extensive catalog, and generous free offerings. She was guided to read and purchase books, e-books, and card decks and to listen to Hay House Radio. She intently followed the World Angel Summit and started communicating with the archangels in earnest. Her studies earned her the title of Certified Angel Intuitive.

She calls on Archangel Michael to keep her family safe and Archangel Raphael to keep them all healthy. She receives daily, author-related guidance, and she is certain she has been hearing from Archangel Gabriel.

One morning, she woke up to the vision of her book cover. She started to google the components, and in no time at all, she was miraculously guided to the artist and the exact vision she had received.

She learned meditation, something she had tried in the 1970s, but she could never calm her mind down and ended up disliking it while her husband has been meditating for over forty years. Under the expert guidance of davidJi through an online course, she learned to rely on mediation as a necessary preparation for her daily writing sessions. Before she starts writing, she follows the guidance of Mike Dooley and is heard yelling "Wahoo!" after meditating to get in an upbeat mood. It works. Kyle Gray fostered her belief in angels. Hay House has many great authors, coaches, and guides who have helped Patty, and they can help you too.

She was guided to have her husband of forty-plus years help her create the ultimate loving world and finalize her first book. Her mom, who entered the spirit world several years ago, had been her editor through life and had encouraged her to take typing and shorthand. She helped her with spelling, grammar, and editing her rewrites; she has been by her side through this journey as her spirit guide. They have the same name and are kindred spirits. Not only is her presence felt, but also, her birthday shows up on the clock continually as does Patty's birth date.

Watch for the next book in the series in which Angie continues her mission for world peace through love.

CPSIA information can be obtained
at www.ICGtesting.com
Printed in the USA
LVOW10*2341210618
580644LV00001BA/15/P